Damasio's Error
and
Descartes' Truth

Damasio's Error and Descartes' Truth

An Inquiry into Consciousness, Epistemology, and Metaphysics

Andrew L. Gluck

Scranton and London
University of Scranton Press

Library of Congress Cataloging-in-Publication Data

Gluck, Andrew Lee.
Damasio's error and Descartes' truth: an inquiry into consciousness, epistemology, and metaphysics / Andrew L. Gluck.
p. cm.
Includes bibliographical references.
ISBN 978-1-58966-127-1 ((pb))
1. Consciousness. 2. Damasio, Antonio R. 3. Social sciences–Philosophy. 4. Philosophy, Medieval. 5. Philosophy, Renaissance. I. Title.
B105.C477G58 2007
126–dc22
2007019061

Distribution:
The University of Scranton Press,
Chicago Distribution Center
11030 S. Langley
Chicago, IL 60628

PRINTED IN THE UNITED STATES OF AMERICA

Dedication

This book is dedicated to the memory and spirit of my teacher Philip Phenix, a true polymath. His work in mathematical physics aroused the admiration of Albert Einstein. He then went on to become an ordained minister, following the spiritual yearnings of his heart. It seems he concluded that the study and teaching of human beings is the best expression of religion and the highest science. He knew so much about almost everything, yet was the most modest and humble man I ever met.

Contents

Acknowledgments

I am indebted to far more people than I can mention for this book. In fact, I hesitate to name anyone for fear that others will be offended. The ideas for the project go back at least to my doctoral dissertation and even further back than that. All those who helped me with that dissertation share much of the credit but none of the blame for what you are about to read. One person stands out, however, and that is O. Roger Anderson. He introduced me to the work of Antonio Damasio. He was also so helpful and generous with his time. I distinctly remember thinking how lucky I was to have a real "hard scientist" on my team. And yet he seemed, by his actions, to recognize more than anyone that the real "hard reality" is the human person.

I would also like to thank Art Gianelli of St. John's University for allowing me to teach the Philosophy of the Human Person course there for so long. My students should also be thanked because ultimately they and their progress are the proof for the validity of my theory.

Also, I thank the many attendees of numerous consciousness conferences with whom I have discussed these subjects. Some of their names I remember but many I have forgotten. All of our discussions were illuminating.

And the members of the Karl Jaspers Society of North America should be thanked, especially those who involved themselves with the *General Psychopathology* and Jaspers' theories of science, personhood and consciousness.

I thank my family for putting up with my psychological and even physical absence while I was absorbed in these preoccupations and particularly my daughter Sarah, who was the impetus for some of these ideas.

It is especially important to acknowledge the help of Jeff Gainey of the University of Scranton Press. He believed in this project and helped guide it to fruition.

Finally, I must thank Antonio Damasio. I used his name, which is the most valuable thing a person has. He must know that I have a great deal of respect for his expertise and knowledge. He must also know that almost all publicity is good. Even though we differ substantially on many matters, I suspect that our motivations are similar and I hope mine are as pure as his.

Preface

The great achievement of consciousness studies is the current acceptability in academic circles of the very concept of consciousness. For a long time it had been considered by many to be a vestigial remnant of pre-scientific philosophy and religion. Behaviorist psychology, logical positivism, analytic philosophy, much of sociology, and of course evolutionary biology had all contributed to a general agreement that the ultimate reality of the human being is physical and consciousness or mental reality must be reducible to physical phenomena. Along came consciousness studies, fueled by new developments in philosophy, psychology, neuroscience, and computer science, and the focus was placed once again on the phenomenon of consciousness. Yet interminable disagreements exist within the field and it is debatable whether much progress has actually been made except perhaps in the dissemination of new empirical findings and the clarification of very basic intuitions. I am hopeful that this book, which of course has a certain bias, will nevertheless be helpful in further clarifying certain issues in the field. While it is rather wide-ranging, it does not purport to be a comprehensive treatment of problems in consciousness studies. Instead it attempts to focus on certain areas that have perhaps been neglected.

This book may seem strange to some. It includes consciousness studies, philosophy of the social sciences, and medieval and Renaissance philosophy. Some may find this combination incongruous. I do not. We have become accustomed to interdisciplinary cooperation between philosophy and science in consciousness studies even if the philosophy of the social sciences has rarely been given much attention. I would argue that any desire to take empirical knowledge into consideration must include the reality of the human person. My insistence that philosophy of the social sciences deserves a prominent place at the table may therefore be allowed. But what does medieval and Renaissance philosophy have to do with consciousness studies?

In our zeal to lay new foundations for knowledge, we often overlook those who preceded us. This is why intellectual history is so important. But perhaps no era has been so ignored by modern thinkers as has the medieval period. Although we have learned a great deal since the Middle Ages, our basic ways of seeing the world were probably born then. I realize that this is a bold statement. Secular thinkers often trace the provenance of their worldview directly to ancient Greece. Religious thinkers may trace theirs to the Bible. Of course, those are the two great sources from which our civilization has sprung. But it was in the much maligned Middle Ages that they definitively came together. And from that union, Western and Islamic civilizations were born.

Compared to some other civilizations, we are still quite young and immature. We probably have much to learn that those older civilizations already know. This may partly explain the great interest in Oriental civilizations and philosophies. Yet we in the West have already performed unimaginable wonders in the world, both physically and ethically/politically. The great new frontier for us is the study of consciousness, and though the East preceded us there, we may have something very important to add to that study that those older civilizations have ignored.

I suspect that in that area our medieval antecedents may be of great help indeed, just as they gave us a basic sense of knowledge and values regarding our concrete existence in the world. That is because what is taken for granted by us in the phenomenon of consciousness was still fresh to them. But why would it have been fresh to them? In order to answer that question, we need to address the apparent fact that at other times the phenomenon of consciousness was taken for granted. Perhaps we are living in such a time. But there is a radical difference between our age and those other ages. While many today fail to fully appreciate the phenomenon of consciousness and even deny its most unique features, many of us are able to react against that view and to do so with the full backing of a long intellectual tradition.

The following are two examples of what I consider a current failure to really appreciate the implications of consciousness. One comes from Eastern thought and the other from the modern scientific worldview. Not too long ago I found myself in the audience of a discussion of Buddhist philosophy and psychology. I was rather amused that people could argue that they, themselves, really don't exist. Perhaps everyone will not share this intuition but it seems to me that arguing *against* selfhood (in contrast to doubting it) is ludicrous if not self-contradictory. If I am right, this may point to something about such assertions that may not always be appreciated, because it does not appear in their standard logical breakdowns. In other words, assertions about selfhood cannot be reduced to assertions about objective entities.

The other example is as follows. On December 14, 2005 two famous biologists, E.O. Wilson and James Watson appeared on the Charlie Rose Show to discuss Darwin. They agreed that he was the most important human being ever to appear on our planet because he showed that there is no designer! If I read this claim correctly, Darwin is the final prophet who has shown that all other prophets were deluded. No wonder that the teaching of evolution has sparked such controversy! The recent interest in the phenomenon of consciousness has led some scientifically minded people to conjecture that it is not some new phenomenon that randomly appeared as a result of human evolution. This is still a hotly debated subject. But if consciousness *is* a fundamental part of reality, those stellar biologists' quasi-religious interpretation of Darwin is wrong and they have confused an adequate scientific *explanation*, which does not require pre-existing consciousness, with an adequate metaphysical *understanding*, which does. I realize that this is a puzzling assertion because many of us have been indoctrinated with the view that science tells us what exists and what does not. I will assert at the outset that, no matter how powerful modern science may be, it leaves out certain aspects of reality. Further arguments for this position will be forthcoming in this book.

I think Descartes can help us here. He (like many of us) thought that consciousness simply presupposed a conscious subject.[1] Perhaps that is why the existence of self followed from the experience of thinking in Descartes' *Cogito ergo sum*. This may explain why the Buddhist arguments struck me as absurd. I also suspect that this tells us something not only about man but about God as well, although Descartes at times denied intuitive knowledge of God.[2] But Descartes was part of a tradition that goes back through the medievals, Augustine, the Neoplatonists, Plato, and the Bible. I believe that that tradition links selfhood with consciousness and makes that linkage crucial for a fuller understanding of reality. Of course, to point to a tradition does not oblige one to accept it. For now, however, it will suffice to simply point and remind readers of the belief system that informs their intuitions.

But given the teachings of Buddhism and some other eastern philosophies, *Cogito ergo sum* is obviously not the only logically conceivable position. I cannot prove Buddhism wrong, just as I cannot prove Descartes right. My hope is that this book will clarify certain issues that are often confused not only by the lay public but by scholars as well. And nothing would be more gratifying to me than that it would lead readers to explore in greater depth some of the range of subjects treated here. For example, this is not an exhaustive study of religious or mystical phenomena. Despite that, what sets it apart from most of the literature in consciousness studies is its willingness to acknowledge the relevance of religion. What do I mean by that?

I believe that it is not only possible but also quite desirable to separate religious belief from science, including social science. Therefore, in constructing a science or sciences of consciousness we generally ought to leave our religious beliefs aside. The failure to do that has doomed many very well intentioned and learned treatises on religion and science. But many of the most contentious issues in consciousness studies are not purely scientific, methodological or epistemological; they are metaphysical. And in that latter area, religious belief is indeed quite relevant. I realize that this is somewhat controversial, but much of the controversy stems from the fact that many scholars in consciousness studies and other fields are pursuing religious or anti-religious agendas without acknowledging or even realizing it. They claim to be doing epistemology or ontology, investigating what we can know or the categories of being, but in reality they are doing a disguised theology and a rather superficial one at that.

But perhaps this book could be accused of doing the same thing. I readily admit that I come to this study with certain pre-conceptions. However, the pluralistic approach championed here should be acceptable to many, holding a wide range of opinions, even if it does not give anyone all that they want. I would hope that it stands firm in not allowing any partial view of human consciousness to disguise itself as the complete picture.

NOTES

1. This is a notoriously complicated subject and I recognize that many interpreters have viewed the *Cogito* as an argument rather than an intuition. For an up-to-date discussion of the various views see Sarkar, 2003.

2. He said that knowledge of God ("short of a miracle") is deduced from "principles of faith" or from "the natural ideas and notions we have." See *the Philosophical Writings of Descartes*, Volume III, p. 331. There are, of course, many possible conceptions of God. The core teaching of the Bible seems to stress the personal and communicative nature of God even more than His omniscience or omnipotence. For an important discussion, see Kugel, 2003.

Introduction

The title of this book derives from a quite influential book by Antonio Damasio entitled *Descartes' Error: Emotion, Reason, and the Human Brain*. Dr. Damasio is one of the foremost neuroscientists of our time and this is only one of many books that he has written. I am not interested in or even capable of criticizing his empirical research and in fact have benefited greatly from it. If, as I suspect, he misinterprets Descartes and Spinoza, I have no great interest in criticizing him for that either. I will, however, attempt to show that his conclusions regarding the implications of research in neuroscience go far beyond the boundaries of empirical science. Dr. Damasio believes that the results of research in thought, consciousness, emotion, bodily changes, and brain states proves conclusively that Cartesian dualism is wrong and therefore body, mind, and emotion ought not to be conceptualized as metaphysically separate entities. His work has aroused a great deal of attention. The *Boston Globe* called the book "an ambitious and meticulous foray into the nature of being." In a later book, entitled *Looking for Spinoza: Joy, Sorrow, and the Feeling Brain*, he goes even further and endorses a metaphysics often called neutral monism: the view that ultimate reality is neither physical nor mental but a neutral substance. In a recent interview he said: "Science is proving Spinoza more current. . . . He intuited the basic mechanism of the emotions."[1] He also considers the following conclusion "Spinozist." "The mind exists for the body, is engaged in telling the story of the body's multifarious events, and uses that story to optimize the life of the organism."[2] Well, despite his undoubtedly altruistic motives, *that* story is indeed optimizing the life of an organism named Antonio Damasio because it is just what so many people want to hear. For example, Jonathan Bate, a Shakespeare scholar, is quoted in the same article. "The division between reason and passion, or cognition and emotion (an opposition that goes all the way back to Aristotle) is, from a neurological point of view, a fallacy."

Those statements, while perhaps true in the context of a limited scientific discourse, have a curiously popular and dogmatic ring to them; they sound like *ex cathedra* pronouncements even if they are made in the name of science. They remind me of Wilson and Watson, who essentially promoted Darwin to the position of supreme prophet. A clear warning sign regarding the relevance of religion is that when Spinoza himself posited an absolute neutral substance he called it both Nature and God.[3] Some say that he only called it God to confer popular respectability upon it. But others consider Spinoza a truly religious thinker, albeit an unorthodox one. Damasio is not the only scientist or philosopher who dares to tread on such dangerous and holy ground; it is actually quite common. I have chosen him as an example because his work is so highly respected.

I believe that this kind of dogmatic metaphysics, which verges on theology, is largely irrelevant to science and science is largely irrelevant to it. Even the lower kind of metaphysics, which investigates the categories of being and is often called ontology, cannot be deduced from scientific investigations, though it can perhaps suggest or stimulate such investigations. For that reason, some ontologies may be more useful than others for particular research projects and I will attempt to give concrete examples. But that is very different from saying the research entails a particular ontology. It is even worse when one extends the conclusion to apply to all of reality. This is one of the main points of this book.

The attempt to base metaphysics on empirical findings is doomed to failure because it presupposes that which it sets out to prove. Empirical findings in the natural sciences are generally couched in physicalist terminology and presuppose the reality of a physical world, at least methodologically. To use those presuppositions to ground metaphysics just doesn't work logically, though it may make good practical sense. This is even admitted by many scientists and philosophers who could be broadly included in the naturalist camp. For example, Colin McGinn has argued for a long time that the *philosophical* problem of consciousness will not be resolved by empirical investigations.[4] Unfortunately, few heed his sage advice.

In addition, empirical findings of the sort that natural scientists work with are only one kind of objective or inter-subjective data. If one really wants to construct a mature metaphysics, either of the lower or higher kind, it is important to include phenomenological data and the results of meaningful connections or *Verstehen*. The inclusion of such data may lead to the suspicion or even the belief that the reality physical science investigates is not the *ultimate* reality. These data also seem to entail belief in selfhood; something that physical science by itself knows little or nothing about.[5] We must of course pay close attention to science but we must also deal with those other issues. As in other highly valued areas of life, we will not easily come to agreement in the study of consciousness. But that does not mean such efforts are futile or meaningless. For example, the question regarding the reality of the individual human person is certainly not meaningless and I hope it is not futile to argue in favor of it. Therefore, I will argue that metaphysics is possible and important even if we will not always agree on it. This is the other main point of the book.

In my view, neutral monism is one possible theological/metaphysical solution to the mind-body problem but in no way is it demonstrable on the basis of empirical evidence. I favor a more pluralistic approach and I think that idealism is another good metaphysical solution. But it seems to me that neither idealism nor neutral monism function very well as epistemological approaches for science. Instead, I offer as alternatives physical monism for the natural sciences and mind-body dualism for the social sciences. They function well as epistemological or ontological approaches in those restricted areas.

Before we go further in describing the pluralistic ontological options, it may be worthwhile to discuss the merits and disadvantages of such an approach. Certainly almost all of us would prefer one universal truth, other things being equal. The double truth theory, wrongly attributed to the Moslem philosopher Averroes, became popular in the late medieval and Renaissance periods. It opposed the more typical medieval attempt to harmonize religion and Aristotle or faith and reason. But, even earlier, we find attempts to articulate the possibility of more than one truth, for example in Maimonides' *Guide of the Perplexed* and the talmudic evaluation of certain contrary or even contradictory opinions as all being "the words of the living God".[6] It seems to me that any attempt to justify more than one truth casts doubts regarding the ultimate truth of each of them. That does not bother me nearly as much as the inability to believe in the ultimate falsity of some views. I would be quite unwilling, for example, to concede the truth of the proposition that the earth is flat. It seems to me that the flat earth theory has indeed been proven false. But regarding some rival scientific, religious, and philosophical views there do seem to be grounds for admitting the possibility of multiple truths (which perhaps is another way of referring to partial truths). I come to this conclusion somewhat reluctantly but it seems to me to be the only way of resolving certain intractable arguments.[7] Having said that, however, we must be cautious in advocating such a view. When we teach children, for example, it may be best to use only one approach to avoid confusion.

What makes neutral monism (or its cousin panpsychism) such an attractive contemporary metaphysical doctrine? Perhaps this has something to do with the rejection of conventional religious belief and the search for an alternative explanatory model. In other words, while science may not need God as a hypothesis, many scientists and others still desperately need something like God and this colors their metaphysical speculations. If one believes in a creating God (as Descartes apparently did) it is relatively easy to argue that the reality God created is really and truly as it appears to us: body and mind. This was especially the case after the scientific discoveries of the seventeenth century freed us from Aristotelian ontological notions that had impinged upon our experience and our epistemology. Mind-body dualism emerged as an ontology as well as a more obvious epistemology. I will go further and suggest it was belief in a supernatural, subjective deity that stimulated and intensified human interiority. That intensification may also have caused the positing of a mind-body problem, something the ancient Greeks never took very seriously in their classical period due to a disregarding of the interior self.[8] This may indeed be one of my more controversial assertions and I would like to elaborate on it now.

It is probably not at all the case in other great civilizations such as those in India or China, (which had their own forms of interiority), but in the West the inner life was incredibly strengthened by biblical religion. One feature that has been noted by people who have done cross-cultural studies is that we in the West tend to view consciousness as intentional, as a subject/object affair.[9] Descartes' discovery of consciousness in the form of doubting led him immediately to the assertion of a self and then of a physical world. Some have said that he didn't really demonstrate the existence of a self but only the existence of doubting consciousness. But our fundamental notion of consciousness in the West involves an ego and a world; it is simply an accepted intuition. That is not necessarily the case in the East, where philosophers have posited pure consciousness without either a self or an objective world. Sometimes we in the West become so fixated upon one pole of consciousness (objective reality) that we practically forget the primacy of the ego. The study and practice of Eastern techniques and philosophies can aid us in breaking out of our bondage to objective physical reality even if it can do little to reduce the importance to us of the ego. But from a historical point of view, that function was performed by biblical religion and Neoplatonism (most often allied with religion). And in fact an argument could be made that our standard account of selfhood and consciousness required both of those spiritual currents. That linkage between religion/philosophy and phenomenal consciousness will be explored in much greater depth later on in this book, but we will have something to say about it now.

KNOWLEDGE, PHILOSOPHY, AND FAITH
The dispute between faith and reason as sources of knowledge goes back to the Middle Ages when fideists sparred with rationalists.

Interestingly, skepticism was most often associated with the anti-rationalist camp in the Middle Ages and a foremost scholar goes so far as to assert that "nothing that I have read from the Renaissance period indicates to me that modern skepticism came through the Aristotelian tradition."[10] While the linkage between skepticism and anti-rationalism may seem counter-intuitive, faith can be viewed as an antidote to skepticism, which itself can be viewed as an illness requiring a cure (especially in an age of faith). A comprehensive rationalism, whether medieval or modern, denies skepticism and denies the need for an antidote.[11] But if rationalism is truly comprehensive, what need is there for faith? That was the question that many of the great medieval rationalists attempted to answer. It is only in the modern period that reason has attempted to go it alone and sometimes it seems that while we have gained much in extensive knowledge, we may have lost an intense interest in the world.[12] An indication of this is that when people do take an extremely intense interest in nature, it is often referred to metaphorically as "religious." There are a multitude of activities which modern people engage in which are so impractical, unhealthy, or painful that one suspects some kind of irrational faith commitment. Examples abound, such as jogging in the ice and snow, keeping wild animals such as wolves and cougars as pets, etc.

One of the roles of philosophy is to explore the limitations of rationality, but once one reaches those boundaries, it may become a poor guide. Reason may also be a poor guide for many mundane tasks. We know from a multitude of studies of decision-making that well adapted people often violate the canons of rationality.[13] This has led to a debate regarding normative rationality vs. successful adaptation. Rationality may not be comprehensive but it becomes uninteresting only when it refuses to acknowledge vital human concerns. I learned many things from my teacher Philip Phenix, but one thing that he said still stands out in my mind: "You can live without knowledge but you can't live without faith." Obviously (from the context) what was meant there was not adherence to any particular doctrine or religious community but something much broader albeit related to faith in its ordinary sense. It refers to a deep-seated conviction that the universe is not hostile or indifferent to the human project. That belief can probably never be confirmed by science. It affirms the efficacy of human reason despite its fallibility and inability to justify itself and confirms our suspicion that the role of teacher is a particularly important one, simultaneously affirming the value of humanity and the value of knowledge of the universe.

In a theistic belief system the question of what is *ultimately* real is often suspended as it pertains only to the nature of the deity: an inquiry that no mortal can adequately answer. Metaphysics in such a system ought to be either provisional or a less than ultimate ontology. It should describe the reality that God created, recognizing that the creation can never be as real as God; or it can attempt to point to the reality of God without really describing it. That is what Descartes did. His system posited three substances: mind, matter, and God. The latter, while more akin to mind than to matter, cannot be known or experienced, as can the other two. And this was the great sin of Spinoza from the point of view of revealed religion. He attempted to collapse the world, mind, and God into one comprehensible and ultimate reality. Like Aristotle, he believed that reality to be eternal. But unlike Aristotle, he apparently saw no need for a God that was separate (at least conceptually). His feelings towards that one great substance seem to have been akin to religious awe and he called it God. Along with that major transgression he committed many little heretical sins, such as denying free will, miracles, and the authenticity of the Bible. Perhaps he was right! Certainly his way of thinking was one of the most remarkable accomplishments of the human mind and one of the most influential (despite the contrary opinion of the aforementioned *New York Times* article). But in my view science can never really decide between Descartes and Spinoza, though it surely can disprove certain beliefs of each.

I have stated that neutral monism and idealism are both acceptable metaphysical doctrines; I will now attempt to show in somewhat greater depth why dualism and physical monism are less good (while admitting their usefulness as scientific methodological principles or limited ontologies).

Let us assume that one believes there is no creating God or that one wants to disregard the possibility altogether. Faced with the *appearance* of mind-body dualism, it seems plausible to assume that reality is ultimately one kind of stuff and not two; therefore some kind of monism would seem to be the best solution. There are three kinds: physicalism, idealism and neutral monism. For reasons that will become clearer in the first chapter, physical monism is not tenable as a metaphysical doctrine, which leaves idealism or neutral monism. Why would the denial or disregarding of the existence of God impel one towards monism? It is logically conceivable that one who does not believe in God could believe in a dualistic or pluralistic universe. This was obviously the case with both the Manicheans and the Gnostics, who did, however, have gods. It is currently, however, more likely that dualistic beliefs would be merely epistemological and not metaphysical, especially for those who are not theists. The same parsimonious impulse that has militated in favor of atheism or monotheism in religious belief and simplicity in scientific theorizing is at work here: the reduction to the simplest good explanation. It is logically possible but somehow dissatisfying to believe that reality ultimately consists of two or more discrete substances. That is why Aristotelian systems tended to exalt either form or matter (usually form) as ultimately substantial or real.

But if one believes there is a creating God, the nature of that deity becomes the ultimate, yet somewhat unanswerable, question. Obviously, few nowadays would argue that the nature of the supreme deity is merely physical and that was not Spinoza's belief either. It is plausible, however, to argue that God is either mind or a neutral substance. Therefore, idealism and neutral monism are the two best metaphysical/theological solutions, whether one believes in God or not.

If my suspicion is correct, Descartes is unpopular today among intellectuals precisely because his metaphysics points toward a more real yet unknowable Being. Spinoza, on the other hand, fits the contemporary scholarly mood much better, as his ultimate reality, whether we call it God or Nature, is indeed knowable. But this is ironic, as Descartes, despite a religious vision in early adulthood, was known to his contemporaries primarily as a scientist, philosopher and mathematician. Spinoza, despite his intense interest in contemporary science, is primarily known as a religious heretic and ethical/political thinker.

The question of physical monism as an adequate methodological model in the natural sciences is dealt with in Chapter One, as are arguments against it as an acceptable metaphysical doctrine. Perhaps I have simplified the matter somewhat but for the sake of argument I am quite happy to concede that this is the proper methodology for the natural sciences and that adding mental features to that ontology complicates things without bringing appreciable benefit. Chapter Two gives an historical overview of how the consciousness problem arose and looks at it from the perspective of aesthetics (and perhaps the humanities in general), which may point towards neutral monism as a solution. Chapter Three presents a kind of idealism that was proposed as a metaphysical solution to ancient theological questions and contrasts it favorably with neutral monism and panpsychism. Chapter Four presents a medieval theistic model that combined neutral monism on the highest levels with idealism on an intermediate level and dualism on the lower ones. It is quite short but despite my efforts to keep it simple, many readers not heavily acquainted with medieval philosophy may find it extremely challenging. It can be skipped. The essential point is that metaphysical systems are complex, and simplicity, while a virtue, often needs to be sacrificed in order to achieve adequacy. Chapter Five sketches the metaphysical views of Descartes and Spinoza and relates them to their respective religious worldviews and to the previously described medieval models. It is not meant to be an exhaustive treatment of these quite complex thinkers. Chapter Six argues for dualism as an epistemological solution in the social sciences. It is crucial to my limited defense of Cartesian dualism; since it seems to me that social science (along with common sense) is the last bastion of dualism.[14] But, like Chapter Four, it is a bit technical, and many readers who are not well versed in philosophy of the social sciences/epistemology and not particularly intrigued by them might be well advised not to bother with it. What one should, however, recognize is the traditional reliance upon the mind-body dichotomy in such sciences as psychology, economics and sociology and how such knowledge contributes to our overall understanding of reality and cannot be profitably reduced to knowledge of physical things. Chapter Seven looks briefly at Damasio's theory of emotions (and the James-Lange theory which inspired it) in light of Karl Jaspers' more phenomenological account. I am hopeful that psychologists would be motivated to deal with this subject in much greater depth. I have appended a conclusion to each chapter, which might help a reader recollect important points or help those who choose not to read them in their entirety.

For those who may think that discussions of other realities (besides the physical) are bizarre and ghostly, I have appended a discussion of Karl Popper's Three Worlds. I hope that scientifically minded readers will benefit from this discussion, particularly since much of it deals with Poppers's collaboration with Sir John Eccles, a leading neurophysiologist. Although Popper never differentiated the social sciences from the natural sciences in terms of methodology, his Three Worlds model may provide a means of doing so. Those who read chapter seven carefully will perhaps recognize that my view of the human sciences requires attention to physicality, consciousness, and culture although the latter two are often not differentiated as Popper does.

NOTES

1. See *The New York Times*, April 19, 2003, D7.
2. Ibid., D9.
3. Although it is not always fully appreciated by modern readers, the very term *nature* has religious significance. Medieval writers such as Thomas Aquinas used the term *natura naturans* as a synonym for God. See Aquinas' *Summa Theologica* IIa-IIae, 85, 6.
4. See McGinn, 1989.
5. See Brentano, 1874, 153–54, where he defined a conscious mental state as one that is directed toward itself.
6. While the literal talmudic quotation (Jerusalem Talmud, Berachot, 1:7, 3b) is not subject to debate, many would deny the attribution to Maimonides of a double-truth position. He never, to my knowledge, explicitly advocates it. Nevertheless, he often does provide more than one view without a deep

endorsement of any particular view—even if he does describe it as the opinion of the faithful or something to that effect. This seems to me to be a concealed way of saying what later thinkers such as Pomponazzi were able to say more openly: at times faith endorses one opinion and reason endorses another. For a description of how Maimonides hides his ambivalent views regarding creation and the eternity of the world, see Gluck, 1998.

7. I was pleased to find that Paul Oscar Kristeller also advocated the use of double or multiple truths in order to resolve controversies between science and the humanities and/or religion. See Kristeller, 1979, 199–200.

8. Professor Richard Sorabji, in a 2004 lecture at the CUNY Graduate Center, spoke of an explosion of interest in the interior self in Greek thought in the first century B.C.E. This certainly implies a relative lack of such interest prior to that period. This also coincides with the collision of Greek thought with Jewish and other oriental religions. He did not, however, address the causes for that increased interest in the self or the inner life, and I cannot claim his support for my hypothesis.

Since completing this book but prior to its actual printing, I was very pleased to read Richard Sorabji's *Self: Ancient and Modern Insights about Individuality, Life and Death*. The same claim regarding intensification of interest in selfhood is made but in a far more nuanced form. He deals with very important subjects that are not substantially addressed in my book. I am still digesting his work and must admit that if I had read it earlier my own book would have been a much better one. For example, I do not discuss psychological continuity vs. ontological identity. Perhaps it is not so important from a neo-Cartesian perspective.

However, Sorabji's notion of ownership pertaining to mental states seems to me to be a bit too broad. I personally *disown* some of my mental states—as when I feel like killing someone. I would hope that if my life continues such feelings could be expunged without any loss of selfhood. This distinction between what happens to me and what I do or think voluntarily is a very important one. That is one reason we may need to revisit the traditional Cartesian distinction between those faculties that pertain to the soul (mind and will) and other faculties that arise from the body (feelings, perceptions, etc.).

9. As an example of the Western attitude, I cite the following question by Louis Dupré in a very important book (Idel & McGinn, 1999, 9). "One of the essays in this collection suggests that self-consciousness is temporarily lost while consciousness remains. This distinction may be impossible to maintain consistently: how could one be at all conscious without being in some way *self*-conscious?"

10. See C.B. Schmitt, 1983, 239.

11. One must distinguish between ancient skepticism, in its Academic or Pyrrhonian forms, and medieval skepticism. Ancient skepticism was viewed as an antidote for a sickness consisting of over-confident belief, and was essentially rational. Medieval skepticism, in its Christian, Moslem, or Jewish versions, was essentially anti-rational and viewed itself as a problem to be resolved through faith. Modern skepticism, perhaps beginning with Spinoza, is another thing altogether, but it would appear to model itself after the ancients. See R. Popkin, 1979.

12. From a purely logical perspective, medieval rationalism may not appear to have required faith, but all of its exponents were men and women of faith and we now know that many of its assumptions were dubious; a modern reconstruction would therefore require a faith commitment.

13. For an excellent collection of articles, see D. Bell, H. Raiffa, and A. Tversky, 1995.

14. I hope the term *last bastion* is not interpreted pejoratively. I see this as a very important defensive position.

Chapter One

The Limits of Physical Monism

One question that this study will try to answer is what kinds of methodology and beliefs about reality are appropriate to various kinds of research. Do all branches of science require the same methodology and if so do they all deal with the same kind of reality? The more narrow focus is consciousness and its place in our views about reality and in the methodologies of the various sciences and other disciplines. While I do discuss reality, I will bypass the question regarding whether science really tells us anything about it. Perhaps it does and perhaps it does not. Intuitively we feel that it does; but so many questions emerge that we cannot really be certain. There are intense debates about this in the philosophy of science. The adherents of Ptolemaic astronomy and Newtonian physics certainly thought that it told them much about reality. We now know that despite the great usefulness of those theories they were wrong about many specifics.

But what about the broader question? Many adherents of quantum mechanics think that it does tell them somewhat scary things about reality; Einstein thought reality could not be like that and therefore rejected it. Obviously, since they contradict one another, many of those metaphysical beliefs of scientists have to be wrong—even more wrong, perhaps, than their scientific theories were. With all that history to look back upon it may be sheer hubris to believe that science, no matter how useful and up to date, tells us much about *ultimate* reality. On the other hand, we do cling to the belief that it tells us *something* about it.

It is clear, for example, that we rarely go to the trouble of studying things that we believe are unreal. Few people attempt to study unicorns *per se* while some do choose to study literature or historical beliefs *about* them. Therefore, although it cannot be proven, there seems to be some natural bias toward the belief that what science describes or explains, while perhaps not the ultimate reality, is real to a degree. And perhaps we should trust that bias to an extent. It may also be perfectly justifiable to believe that science can tell us that some things are unreal. But we surely cannot assume that anything a particular science fails to deal with cannot therefore be real.

At times scientists prefer to describe their method as involving *natural* rather than *physical* explanations. I think that this attempt to include certain theoretical fictions that should not be thought of as physical objects does not address the ontological question. It seems to me that all theoretical explanations in the natural sciences ultimately are justified by occurrences in the physical world (including the laboratory). And what makes *supernatural* explanations suspicious in science? For example, we often read about experiments regarding prayer or mental telepathy that often have mixed results. But let us do a mental experiment and imagine that most studies do indeed show the efficacy of prayer for physical healing.

How would scientists interpret those results? There seem to be three likely alternatives. The first would be to conclude that prayer somehow affects the physical world directly and promotes healing in a way that we don't yet understand. The second would be to conclude that God responds to the prayers and then affects the physical world (also in a way that we don't understand). The third would be to simply say that mind and matter are ultimately the same thing and therefore the results of these experiments should not surprise us.

I am sure that the second alternative would be rejected because not all scientists believe that there is a God. Most scientists would prefer the first explanation. But what if the first explanation were ruled out by all available scientific knowledge. For example one could imagine locking those who are praying in some very remote location and shielding the sick people from any awareness of them. I think that scientists would still opt for the first explanation. Perhaps after many such experiments in many disparate fields came up with similar results they might begin to consider the third option. The reason should be obvious. Most natural science depends upon physical mechanisms to explain such events as healing. Saying that the physical and the mental are the same thing doesn't really pull any explanatory weight.

I will assert at the outset that the methodological and epistemological approach that fits natural science best is physical monism but that such a methodology is perfectly compatible with the belief that there are other kinds of reality that natural science cannot study. I will spend little further time or effort convincing the reader that this is the best epistemological/methodological doctrine for physical science. Perhaps there are quantum physicists and philosophers who will disagree with that as a broad epistemic principle and many people who write about science and religion may not like it. But for the vast majority of research programs in natural science it is valid and it remains the opinion of most natural scientists. It is certainly true that recent discoveries on the subatomic level raise interesting and serious questions regarding the *ultimate* nature of physical reality but those were questions that philosophers were raising from time immemorial. It is also quite possible that a better model will emerge eventually. But there is not yet any methodological model in natural science that can compete with physical monism, especially over the broad range of natural sciences such as biology, chemistry, geology, etc. (though perhaps excluding physics).

The question arises, however, as to whether physical monism constitutes an adequate ontology. My tentative answer is that in certain limited areas of the things that physical science studies, it does, but that we run into problems when we try to integrate that knowledge with other areas of our lives. It is quite tempting, therefore, to turn to neutral monism as a solution. But when you look closely at that solution it may create more problems than it solves. One possible problem is metaphysics disguising itself as science— as when people use the uncertainties and perplexities of quantum mechanics to jump to unwarranted conclusions about ultimate reality. Another problem is that one can pay lip service to neutral monism but allow physical monism to pull all of the weight. The first problem is a major one because, in my opinion, scientific knowledge can't entail an ontology and even less so can scientific perplexity.[1] The second problem is a violation of parsimony, which goes against accepted scientific protocol but is perhaps less of a logical or philosophical problem. Therefore, if one needs a limited ontology, physical monism is acceptable and certainly it is quite acceptable as a methodological principle in the physical sciences.

When it comes to the social or human sciences, however, it is quite doubtful that physical monism works well even as a methodological principle. What I am attempting to do here is not to show what would constitute a valid methodology in those sciences but simply to reveal the inadequacy of physical monism as a universally valid ontology. I would like to quote from Neil Carlson's excellent introductory textbook on physiological psychology in order to give a flavor of what I am alluding to: that the methodology appropriate to natural science is not fully adequate for use in the social sciences.

> Monism is the belief that reality consists of a unified whole and, thus, that the mind is a phenomenon produced by the workings of the body. . . . What we call "mind" is a consequence of the functioning of the body and its interactions with the environment. The mind-body problem thus exists only as an abstraction. . . .

> The question of consciousness suggests another issue: *determinism* versus *free will*. . . . Because a belief in free will implies that the mind is not constrained by physiology, it is a form of dualism. This belief is unacceptable in the laboratory. . . .

> Certainly a belief in determinism is a belief in monism. But in addition, it is a belief that the world is an orderly place where each event is determined by the events that precede it.[2]

This quotation raises many provocative issues, not all of which can be resolved in this study. I find myself in agreement with some of the things that Carlson said but I also find it somewhat simplistic and misleading. If he is only referring to laboratory methodology in physiological psychology, that is fine, but I think his language can easily be interpreted in a much broader meta-physical sense. Even in the purely physical sciences such as chemistry or geology it is questionable whether such statements should be made in an ultimate metaphysical sense. In fact, there is a real possibility that, if taken metaphysically, such a statement is self-contradictory, as I will now attempt to show.

In order to see the ultimate incoherence of this as a general metaphysical view we need to apply it to areas of reality where it clearly does not fit. This is quite obviously the case in psychology where such paradigms as behaviorism, physicalism (in the narrow sense), or artificial intelligence are indeed often employed but, in my view, with bad results. The desire to equate consciousness with behavior, neural activity, or information processing all stem from this particular worldview. Others have written quite exhaustively on the scientific worldview that excludes qualia (discrete items of phenomenological consciousness) from its view of reality.[3] It has been called positivism, materialism, physicalism (in the broad sense), etc. No matter what we call it, however, as an onto-logical view it seems intimately related to the quite valid method-ological view called naturalism. It is possible, however, that to the extent to which that methodological view denies the reality of phenomenal consciousness, it is incoherent.

Let us assume for now that naturalistic nomological/causal explanation is indeed the true methodology of natural science.[4] Some would argue that this method is also the correct one for the human sciences. They say that its success in the natural sci-ences is so impressive that we can confidently assume no other things exist aside from those described by it. Those who make that claim would like to elevate this methodology to a universally valid metaphysical system. But such a universal system ought to be able to comprehend its own reality as well as that of physical structures. One could begin by inquiring regarding the purpose of science. Perhaps the least that could be claimed is that it helps to predict events. Since, however, the forecasting of events must exclude any experiential or phenomenological quality (according to the naturalistic method), it is perhaps defined as a prediction occurring at a certain point in time followed by a decision at a later time as to the accuracy of that prediction. But those predictions and decisions are verbal actions. When we attempt to assign some meaning to them it may become obvious that meaning is dependent upon phenomenal consciousness. But phenomenal consciousness according to the naturalist paradigm doesn't really exist! So it would seem that science is not meaningful at all.[5] The consequence of over-reliance on the method of natural science seems to be that the very activities of the scientists are deprived of meaning! Hence, even the comprehensibility of natural science may presuppose phenomenal consciousness.[6]

One of the problems in reconciling mind and body is that some people try to do it on the cheap. They argue that of course consciousness exists and then proceed to explain it away in terms of behavior or brain functioning. Apparently, this is less controversial than simply denying the reality of phenomenal consciousness. I don't know too many people who do the reverse but it is theoretically possible. One could argue that of course the physical world exists and then proceed to explain it away as a manifestation of ideas, as idealists have often done. The reason why that strategy is seldom employed is that it simply wouldn't work as a scientific explanatory device even if it could be plausibly argued as a metaphysical doctrine. We live in a scientific age and that is one very good reason why idealism is problematic.

This leads to another important point. There is a pervasive aspect of our thinking that I will refer to as the physicality bias. This may militate against idealism even more than science. Even when we try to conceptualize reality in a neutral monist or panpsychist fashion, we almost always end up thinking of it as physical matter. This is perhaps almost inevitable in a creature that evolved in a physical universe even if unusual mystics and philosophers such as Plato, Plotinus, and Berkeley, who think quite differently, influence us from time to time.

And explaining mental phenomena in terms of physical phenomena does work to a certain extent. I don't think that it explains nearly enough of the phenomena of *human existence* to be a convincing scientific research program, however. I have also attempted to show that it is incoherent as an ultimate metaphysical claim. Nevertheless, we must admit that it has a certain scientific value and can lead to useful behavioral and technological discoveries, aside from simply being our default way of thinking.

If physical monism is not a good metaphysics, what is? In chapters two and three I will consider two alternatives: neutral monism and idealism. Idealism makes sense from certain theological perspectives as it can be applied to both God and the world. But, as I argued previously, it has the distinct disadvantage of appearing to conflict with empirical science. I will present another type of idealism that does not conflict too badly with science. But I readily admit that standard accounts of idealism do conflict horribly with the scientific worldview. Of course one can be a good scientist and a metaphysical idealist. It is not only possible but there have been a number of good examples.[7] Nevertheless, there is a certain cognitive dissonance in investigating the physical world yet not believing that it is real. One could fall back on the belief that science doesn't really describe reality but only phenomena; yet the cognitive dissonance remains.

Neutral monism is far superior as a metaphysical view because it allows for the reality of both the physical and mental worlds. This is also the most acceptable view from the perspective of aesthetics, as I will attempt to show in chapter two. It may not be as theologically satisfying as idealism but it can certainly be reconciled with theism and with dualism on lower levels of reality. In chapter four I will present an historical example of how that was done in the Middle Ages. It has the added advantage of having the most appeal to people who don't believe in a creator God or don't want to consider the question. In other words, if one considers the universe as we know it (in a very broad sense) to be eternal or not to have a beginning, neutral monism seems to fit best with that belief. That is because, unlike physical monism, it explains the phenomenon of consciousness while not requiring a belief in the creation of matter.

CONCLUSION

Physical monism is currently the best epistemological model in the natural sciences. As such, it naturally suggests itself as an ontological model as well. In a limited sense this is appropriate. But physical monism does not work well as an ultimate metaphysical view, whether or not one believes in a creating God. Neutral monism has certain advantages as an ultimate metaphysical view but all too often it gets conflated with physical monism or, as I often call it, *physicalism in the broad sense*. Idealism is another viable candidate as an ultimate metaphysics, especially for those who believe in a creating God. It suffers from the distinct disadvantage, however, of appearing to conflict with science.

NOTES

1. Some will disagree and argue that scientific knowledge does indeed imply ontology, but few will assert that scientific perplexity can.
2. Carlson, 1994, 4–5. He admits, however, that he cannot prove his determinist/monist position.
3. One of the best that I have read is Stubenberg, 1997. I agree with him that physicalism as an ontological view eliminates qualia and phenomenal consciousness.
4. We will assume for now that such a methodology implies physical monism as a limited ontology. But perhaps it does not. There does, however, seem to be a deep affinity between the two views. And it seems that whenever traditional rules of causality don't seem to work, ontology is called into question.
5. When I speak of *meaning* I am not referring to a normative concept but to a value-free one as in the question: What does that mean to you? It may also have been noticed that my argument presupposes that phenomenal consciousness is a necessary condition for that kind of meaning, and not just in science. Some disagree with this. I grant that it rests on an intuition that not everyone shares. The following thought experiment might distinguish between those who do and do not. Imagine a language that no one understands and a proposition written in that language. Is it meaningful? From a certain linguistic point of view it is; nevertheless it is not meaningful *to* anyone. Likewise, if you eliminate phenomenal consciousness, science (as well as every other kind of discourse) is not meaningful to anyone.

6. Some regularities in nature are not comprehensible. But going back to the Islamic Kalam, through Hume and Dilthey, there have been philosophers who argued that regularities in nature are never comprehensible. This leaves two possibilities. If one accepts those arguments, natural science is only comprehensible by reference to some other form of knowledge—theology for example. But whatever the ultimately comprehensible science might be, it can only be comprehended by one possessing phenomenal consciousness. It has recently been brought to my attention that a quite similar argument was made by Norman Malcolm (1968). But some quite formidable thinkers detach meaning from consciousness as when they deny that an intentional state must be a conscious state. See Searle, 1983, 3. Technically they may be correct but, as Searle points out, a non-conscious intentional state must be at least capable of being brought into consciousness.

7. Most of these examples come from one field—physics. That is because the highly abstract, mathematical nature of physics lends itself to idealism much more than the other sciences do.

Chapter Two

The Consciousness Problem and How We Got to It

> The defining function of the artist is to cherish consciousness.
>
> —Max Eastman

In this chapter, I will attempt to look at consciousness from a historical perspective, sometimes using aesthetics as an illustrative device. Some kind of neutral monism will emerge as a good metaphysical solution and I will argue that aesthetics provides a better justification for it than does science, albeit an imperfect justification. Neutral monism also partly explains the fact that ancient philosophers often failed to discern a mind-body problem. If reality is one substance, it makes perfect sense that people could neglect certain aspects of it just as none of the blind men knew everything about the elephant. But if reality consists of two completely distinct categories of being, how on earth could intelligent people have missed one of them? Neutral monism will also be seen to explain the constant tension in art between objective representation and subjective appearance or abstract expression, and it explains the unified nature of the aesthetic experience.[1] Nevertheless, that phenomenon could probably also be explained by other metaphysical or ontological schemes. As in the sciences, the study of art or aesthetics does not logically entail acceptance of any particular ontological belief but some such positions may be more useful than others. It could be that neutral monism is a quite adequate viewpoint in the humanities generally since all cultural artifacts have a material component as well as a mental one.[2]

Natika Newton states: "phenomenal consciousness is *sui generis*. Nothing else is like it *in any way at all*, because anything other than phenomenal consciousness is unconscious, and hence not like anything."[3] Since the publication of Nagel's article "What is it like to be a bat?" in 1974, that has been the standard treatment of phenomenal consciousness in philosophical literature. And since nothing else can be like it at all, either phenomenal consciousness exists *sui generis* or it really doesn't exist at all.

It should be noted that other interpretations of consciousness avoid that stark choice. This phenomenal concept of consciousness, as completely distinct from objective physical reality, generates what is often called the consciousness problem. It is a dilemma. On the one hand, as we have seen, it is unfashionable to adopt a Cartesian dualist position and physical monism seems the only tenable methodological position in the natural sciences. But on the other hand, consciousness is just so different from everything else!

Is that *sui generis* notion an intuition that almost everyone would agree with nowadays? It seems that it is. Of course there are many who deny it as an ultimate explanation but even most of them would probably admit that the real truth of the matter is counterintuitive. (Yet there were periods in human history when that would not have been a widely accepted intuition at all.)[4] And despite that intuition there are very few modern thinkers who would be willing to completely divorce consciousness from physical reality. Most of us would have great difficulty imagining how consciousness could exist without a brain, for example. We also tend to think that there is a strong connection between intelligence and consciousness leading some to a more epistemic view of experience.

The cognitive dissonance created by these two notions of consciousness or experience—as *sui generis* on the one hand and as irremediably linked to the physical world on the other—have impelled some to espouse neutral monism or panpsychism as metaphysical solutions to the problem. Whether those two positions amount to the same thing in the end is a problem that will not detain us here.[5] I suspect, however, that neutral monism satisfies some of our aesthetic intuitions as they have developed historically. I will also address the processes of intellectual history that produced a consciousness problem and exemplify them by reference to aesthetic theory.

If anything can capture the elusive notion of phenomenal consciousness it is perhaps our conception of the beautiful. Indeed, the very term *aesthetics* comes from the Greek verb *aesthanesthai*, meaning *to perceive*.[6] Up until the eighteenth century the term *aesthetics* was still used for perception or sensation and its current use only dates from the German philosopher A.G. Baumgarten in 1750.[7] I will review the way ancient Greek thinkers looked at consciousness and contrast it with the way medieval and early modern Western thinkers viewed it. I am not concerned here with more contemporary thinkers as the consciousness problem had already been posited and I am not attempting to resolve that problem but simply to show how it arose in the first place.

Regarding aesthetics, I will try to show how the concept of beauty and sublimity changes with varying notions of consciousness. We will see that, for the ancients, the touchstone of beauty was an objective quasi-mathematical standard that mirrored their understanding of the more significant aspects of the human mind. Later on, in the Middle Ages, aesthetics would be subordinated to religious experience. Experience, of course, always has an individual and subjective aspect even when it is put into the service of an abstract ideology. Or perhaps it is more accurate to say that we in the West tend to interpret consciousness as the experience of a particular person. That emphasis on individual experience would continue through the Renaissance and into Romantic art and, later on, would overwhelm objective standards of physical reality. This first became obvious in Impressionism where the emphasis was placed on what the visual senses actually experience.

The reaction to Impressionism, whether from Cezanne, Van Gogh, Matisse, or Picasso, stressed art as an original creation of the mind rather than the senses alone. Hence the emphasis on conscious individual experience, whether sensory, emotional, or intellectual, is the central motif of all modern art.[8] This confluence of the physical, emotional and intellectual in the actual history of art may somehow remind us of Damasio's arguments for neutral monism and against Cartesian dualism. But we have argued previously that empirical data cannot provide a firm basis for metaphysical speculation.

Perhaps aesthetic theory is a somewhat more solid foundation. We know that aesthetic experiences provide many people with something like a religious or metaphysical experience. This can occur either in artistic experience or in the experience of nature. While such experiences on their own cannot logically support firm metaphysical conclusions, they may provide better evidence than the worldview of the special sciences, which so often leave us dissatisfied and unfulfilled.[9] In other words, the actual aesthetic experience may teach us more about consciousness than historical or psychological discussions of that experience. While we remain somewhat skeptical of all metaphysical speculation, if any experience is to function as at least a necessary condition for such conclusions it must carry within itself a great deal of persuasive satisfaction. Therefore, aesthetic experience (whether natural or artistic) may provide a good foundation for metaphysical speculation, at least psychologically if not logically. Keeping that in mind, the reader should accept the very limited nature of this discussion.

Consciousness became a major theoretical problem in the early modern period with thinkers like Descartes and Locke, but the problem was brewing in medieval thought in a way that it had not for the ancients. am certainly not suggesting that phenomenal consciousness did not exist in the ancient world. If it exists now it existed then (though perhaps in a less intense form), and if it is an illusion now it surely did not exist then. What I am suggesting, however, is that it was hardly noticed then in comparison to how it preoccupies us now. One reason is that for the ancients phenomenal consciousness was often interpreted as being essentially something else. This stands in stark contrast to the more modern intuition previously described.

THE ANCIENT VIEWS

The Hebrew Bible has a rather large number of words to describe human life, consciousness, mind, etc. The prime candidates for what we would call the soul, however, are two variations of the same word: *leb* and *lebob*. Those words which literally refer to the heart or to the heart cage often denote the mind or will, in contrast to other words that tend to describe the life force, emotions, imagination, etc.[10] The word *nephesh*, which most literally means breath and in later periods came to denote the soul, coincides in the Bible more with our notion of life force. It is peculiarly related to the blood, is often used in reference to animals and denotes numbers of living things. It may also denote emotion or vitality. For example in *Deuteronomy* 6,5 we read "Thou shalt love the Lord thy God with all thy heart (*lebob*) and with all thy soul (*nephesh*) and with all thy might." The translation, while standard, is not good and should indeed be reversed because you do not love with your physical heart and for us heart is a metaphor for emotion but in the Bible *lebob* does not mean emotion and *nephesh* does not mean soul.[11]

The Bible expresses its interest in human life and subjectivity with an extremely complex array of descriptors especially considering the fact that biblical Hebrew is a generally impoverished language with its small number of words and its difficulty describing many mundane aspects of life. It seems strange that so many of those scarce words should serve to signify what we might term the subjective pole of human experience. The basic message that this may convey is that objective reality depends utterly upon a living subjective Being, in whose image humankind was created. Nevertheless, in comparison to Greek thought, the Bible does not concern itself very much with the human mind and its relationship to physical reality. It takes it for granted that humans have the power to cognize—as when Adam is given the task of naming all of the animals—but it shows very little interest in the actual mechanics of perception, imagination, reason, and knowledge.

In the Bible, emotion (especially negative emotion) is an essential aspect of the inner life of the individual. Furthermore, there is very little discussion of immortality and most often the accepted view of it is quite skeptical. Perhaps discussions of immortality were reminiscent of the despised Egyptian culture. There is also little interest in dissecting the human soul into animal passions, reason, imagination, etc. Although certain words more or less typically are used to signify each faculty, there appears to be a great deal of overlap between the different words. Hence one could perhaps be justified in saying that the biblical view of the human person is rather inchoate and quite remote from our more highly developed concept, despite its intense interest in human subjectivity.

The question naturally arises regarding whether the ancient Hebrews really identified consciousness with the wind, breath, kidneys, gullet, heart, etc. Unfortunately, we will probably never know the intricate nuances of many biblical expressions and we certainly can't know the entire range of beliefs in that era regarding consciousness. We still speak of knowing something *in our gut* or speaking *from the heart* but few of us take those expressions literally just as few of us take the anthropomorphic descriptions of God in the Bible literally. And that may be precisely the point. In ancient times (even in the Middle Ages) many people really did believe that God had a physical body just as they identified consciousness with certain physical phenomena. We find here, as is usual with biblical culture, intensity of interest and utmost seriousness of commitment without a great deal of analysis. For a more analytical approach we must turn to ancient Greece.[12]

The pre-Socratic Greek view of the human soul, and particularly the Homerian one, is quite complex and difficult to decipher.[13] There has been a great deal of discussion regarding belief in immortality of the soul in Homer's time and the consensus seems to be negative.[14] Some pre-Socratic views will be looked at shortly through the eyes of Aristotle. It is generally believed that Pythagoras took a special interest in the human soul and Plato may have obtained some of his views from Pythagorean sources. At any rate, Plato (or perhaps Socrates) really fixed the focus of Greek thought on the human soul. Yet when we look closely at Plato's writings it is impossible not to notice that his views are as remote from ours as are those in the Bible. Yet no one could accuse him of not being analytical.

When Plato attempted to prove the immortality of the soul in the *Phaedo*, one of the ways he went about it was by asserting that the Forms are eternal. He then noted a resemblance between the soul and the Forms and concluded that the soul must also be eternal.[15] This is a quite remarkable procedure from the standpoint of modern thought, because it is not at all clear to us what those Forms are and why we resemble them.

When students are first introduced to Plato there is a tendency for them to equate the Platonic Forms with ideas. They must be warned that the Platonic Forms are objective entities and not ideas in someone's mind. Nevertheless, one of the most convenient ways to approach it for many people is to equate the Forms with ideas in the mind of God or in a *Logos*, as such thinkers as Philo of Alexandria and future generations of Neoplatonists did. Philo did that for religious reasons though he might have been capable of comprehending Plato's theory. For a Jew of that period no reality could supercede God—not even the eternal Forms. And if there is a resemblance between those Forms and human beings it is because humans have thoughts just as God has thoughts and therefore the Forms must originate as the thoughts of God. Unfortunately, that falsifies the Platonic view somewhat because, for Plato, the Forms are eternal and stand by themselves without any need for positing a divine mind, even though he might have believed in one, and certainly spoke of one.

Modern students tend to be baffled by Plato's theory and interpreting the Forms as divine ideas takes them even further away from it. The reason that we moderns (like Philo) find it convenient to think of the Forms as ideas is that we are wedded to a notion of subjectivity that the ancient Greeks simply were not. This is a point that bears some repetition because we often assume that all people experience their humanity in the same way. Yet some are inured to death and suffering while others are not. Some see no problem with exposure of infants, human sacrifice, the chopping off of heads and limbs, etc. This is a subject that can lead in many different directions. My only reason for stressing it here is that we cannot assume that ancient peoples saw the world and themselves as we do, and understanding that may save us from many futile inquiries.

This general lack of interest in subjectivity in ancient Greece may also explain how it is that Plato views the activities of the soul as quite dependent upon physical changes. In the *Timaeus*, Plato describes the soul as being moved by physical forces and even being deluded by them. That is how he explains the fact that the soul is foolish when it is young (despite its pre-existence).[16] Some take such statements of Plato allegorically or even jokingly, as when he states that those who misuse their powers of reason will be reincarnated as an animal with a long snout in order to accommodate their misshapen soul.[17] Undoubtedly, later generations of Platonists were embarrassed by such statements and did not take them literally.

In the *De Anima*, Aristotle reviews the attitudes of previous Greek thinkers regarding the soul in a fairly comprehensive manner. Anaxagoras did seem to distinguish between mind/soul and matter but there were few others who did. Both Democritus and the Pythagoreans thought that the soul had something to do with respiration. Democritus thought soul was a fine-grained kind of matter and its atoms were of spherical shape. Thales viewed soul as a motive force like magnetism. Diogenes thought that the soul was air. Heraclitus considered soul to be a warm exhalation. Alcmaeon said that the soul was immortal because it resembled such immortal things as the moon, sun, planets, etc. Aristotle also mentioned some more "superficial" thinkers, all of whom held soul to be some physical substance. He concluded that only Anaxagoras held soul to "have nothing in common with anything else."[18] One might perhaps conclude from that statement that even his teacher Plato did not hold such a view and we have already seen that Plato seemed to view the soul as akin to the Forms.[19]

One might also recall that for Plato the opinion of Anaxagoras that mind is the creator of all other things was just a verbal formula not matched by rigorous thought.[20] And it was that perceived failure of Anaxagoras' theory that led to his theory of Forms. That theory explained the origin of everything (mind and matter) as a result of the eternal Forms even if the human soul seemed somewhat more akin to those forms. In other words, Plato seems to have rejected the notion that body and soul are completely distinct phenomena while nevertheless recognizing some dissimilarity and the need for some superior principle (form) in order to understand both of them. He was not a materialist, idealist or dualist but (to coin a new expression) a formist.

Aristotle makes another very revealing statement in the *De Anima*. He distinguishes between those who view soul as the originator of movement and those who view it as the ability to know or perceive reality. The latter, according to Aristotle, all identify soul with "the principle or principles of nature." He then goes on to quote Empedocles.

For 'tis by Earth we see Earth, by Water Water,

By Ether Ether divine, by Fire destructive Fire,

By Love Love, and Hate by cruel Hate.[21]

It might be noted that the soul can be viewed as the originator of motion, as the knower or perceiver *and also as the conscious experiencer.*[22] How could he have missed the latter?

Another example of the attitude of the ancient Greeks is found in the views of Aristotle himself. In the *De Anima* he asserts the existence of a common sense that is the source from which we are conscious of our mental and sensory processes. It is interesting to see how he demonstrates this. He begins by defining *sense* as "what has the power of receiving into itself the sensible forms without the matter." Sensory objects affect all bodies but only the senses can observe the results of being so affected.

It might be thought that there is a sense organ that receives these "common sensibles," but Aristotle insists that there is no sixth sense but a general sensibility that enables us to receive them. We can, for example, compare the objects of two completely different senses: the white and the sweet for example. It is this general sensibility that stands aside from the special senses.

The special senses actually take in the forms of their objects but this special sensibility does not. So the common sense only informs us that we are having an experience; it does not tell us what it is like to have that experience. The general sensibility that makes us conscious that we are being so affected is, therefore, nothing more than a recognition of that which objectively exists in the special senses. In a sense, the perceiver becomes that which he or she perceives because the proper or sensible form (the actuality of the perceived thing) is received by the soul in perception just as the intelligible form is received in thought. That is somewhat different from the previous thinkers who held that the soul is *by nature* like the thing that is perceived, but it will indeed turn out that the soul is also like what it perceives because it is also a form (of the living body).

There is, however, for Aristotle another post-sensational faculty that might come closer to what we call experience or consciousness. That faculty is imagination—*phantasia* in Greek. That word, according to Aristotle, is derived from *phaos* or light. Some of the characteristics of imagination are that it retains sensory images, it most often is false, and it is under the control of the person to a certain extent. It is that retentive aspect that could allow for consciousness. According to this intuition, we can only be conscious of that which can be retained long enough to take another look at. A purely momentary sensation would not really be consciousness. Hence imagination and memory play a crucial role in consciousness.

But some people will not agree with that intuition and argue that there are altered states of *consciousness* in which almost all mental faculties such as imagination and memory are interrupted. Some animals, according to Aristotle, are governed by imagination but others lack the capacity and it is questionable whether any of them have the control over this faculty that humans have. So of the two post-sensational Aristotelian faculties that might qualify as the seat of experience, common sense and imagination, the latter is the more likely candidate if we are interested in the qualitative aspect of experience.

Therefore, it is probably wrong to argue, as some have, that a thinker as great as Aristotle completely failed to recognize phenomenal consciousness. But it *can* be said that imagination (consciousness) for Aristotle does not possess any of the exalted connotations that we moderns often associate with human experience.[23] It is a relatively low-level cognitive faculty and not highly esteemed. "For perception of the proper objects is always true, and occurs in all animals, whereas it is possible to think falsely and no animal without reason possesses thought. For phantasia is different from either perceiving or thinking, though it is not found without perception, nor judgment without it."[24]

Perception has the virtue of always correctly reproducing the perceived object. Thought, the most exalted faculty, can be false and if so the most likely culprit is the imagination, which acts as an intermediary between perception and thought. But aside from the problems of human cognition, for Aristotle there was no inherent mind-body dichotomy. Both his view of the physical and the mental would not allow for that. As Burnyeat put it so succinctly: "To be truly Aristotelian, we would have to stop believing that the emergence of life or mind requires explanation."[25] This will turn out to be perfectly normal once we understand more about the ancient Greek mind.

As we have seen, the ancient Greeks tended to objectify subjective experience as something out there, so there really was no consciousness problem to be resolved. Even those thinkers who may have recognized phenomenal experience did not accord it a great deal of significance. This attitude reveals itself clearly in the visual arts. For us, a work of art is a unique specimen that derives its significance from the *individuality* of its creator as well as from the *unique experiences* provided to its viewers.[26] This was not the view of the ancient Greeks at all. For them visual art was more like a craft and had about it the somewhat stigmatized aura of *banausos*.[27] It had no great cognitive value and at best it was good imitation.[28] This is evident in Plato;[29] we also find in Plato a then prevalent belief (which he to his credit rejected) that beauty is synonymous with usefulness or power.[30] In other words, the ancient Greeks could not simply trust their sensations when it came to beauty. It would have to pass some kind of objective test. And this was the case despite the fact that they considered sight to be the most exalted of all the senses!

The famous quotation of Vitruvius is indicative of the classical attitude towards the visual arts. "Painting gives the image of what is or can be." He went on to exclude that which "being only a product of the imagination, does not exist, cannot exist and never will exist." Poetry, music, theatre, and philosophy were much more highly esteemed because they were thought to more closely approach the abstract form. Beauty for the Greeks was not in the eye of the beholder; it was out there in proportion and symmetry. The creative artist who saw things differently and expressed that perception in creative work was not esteemed at all but condemned.

The individuality of the ancient Greeks, an area in which they were pioneers, centered on agonal competition. The individual defined himself not in his uniqueness but in the superiority in the display of some abstract principle. A look at the ancient Greek heroes reveals them to be isolated individuals at the mercy of an antagonistic god and/or a cold, inexorable fate. With no one to turn to for help, how could they possibly understand the uniqueness and value of their inner lives? In all aspects of life it was the abstract principle and not the unique individual that reigned supreme. Symmetry as an abstract objective quality was the touchstone of beauty and no better example could be found than the perfect human body, which tended to be the male body because beauty was not easily associated with weakness. It is said that Zeuxis the Greek artist who painted the portrait of Helen of Troy had to look at many beautiful women before he was able to paint that masterpiece. That is perhaps because women were identified with matter, individuality and weakness. The male principle, on the other hand, was something much more abstract and universal: Form.

The Stoics took that abstract notion of symmetry to an extreme and Plotinus took them to task for confining beauty to symmetry. He himself argued for a more experiential view of beauty. I think that this was a general trend in the Hellenistic and Roman periods when the ideals of the ancient Greeks collided with oriental cults. The most influential of those cults, of course, was Judaism, which placed at the center of its worldview an omnipotent, personal, *subjective* Being.[31] Judaism and Christianity both rejected any finite objectification of God with the one exception that will be discussed shortly. This prohibition of objectification, while never fully understood by the multitude, points in the direction of a God who is subjective and/or transcends subjectivity/objectivity. The one exception, of course, is humanity as the image of God. We find this concept in the very beginning of the Bible. We also find in Isaiah 6:1, and even more explicitly in Ezekiel 1:26–28, mystical visions of God likened to a human form. In Christianity this identification of man and God is extended in its scope yet delimited to the man Jesus and his subjectivity (especially his suffering) pointing to the subjective reality of God.

Christianity imported the idea of a subjective God into Western civilization. And as would be expected, those human traits viewed as imitations of a divine reality were exalted. Interestingly, however, even a Neoplatonic thinker such as Plotinus, who was repelled by the notion of a suffering God, argued for a more experiential approach. He argued, more generally, that through training one could lessen the dependence of even the lower soul on the body.[32] Indeed, for Plotinus the higher soul (which is the real person) has little at all to do with the body. It is difficult to get at the precise historical causes for this change, but it may be that the collision of Hellenism and oriental culture produced a shift towards individual self-awareness that manifested itself not only in religious and aesthetic phenomena but also in Hellenistic leadership cults.

There were, of course, those who persisted in the tendency of Greek thought to subordinate subjectivity to objective reality (whether formal or physical). Perhaps the best example is Galen who insisted upon viewing the qualities of the soul as the result of physical events.[33] Alexander of Aphrodisias, an Aristotelian scholar and a rival of Galen, did not like the traditional Greek identification of body and soul and introduced a concept of supervenience. Admitting that physical changes have profound effects upon the soul, he nevertheless insisted that the two are quite different things.[34] This shift towards interiority would become even more apparent as the invading Germanic tribes entered the center stage of history, destroying the Roman Empire but absorbing much of its civilization.[35]

AUGUSTINE

At the very time of those Germanic invasions there lived a man who would move Western thought inwardly in a decisive manner; his name was Saint Augustine. For Augustine, the mental processes of perception are identical with imagination except for the presence of attention. That latter mental faculty prevents the imagination from pursuing its own creative proclivities and binds it to the sensory activities of the corporeal organs. But unlike the ancient Greeks (Plato in particular) from whom he learned so much, consciousness or imagination is no longer dependent upon sensory images; it now has a life of its own. In contrast to Aristotle, imagination is not only retentive and imitative of external sensory perception but is inherently creative and only accidentally attached to the organs of sense.

Also worthy of mention is Augustine's expanded concept of memory as an internal divine illumination of the mind. For the ancient Greeks, memory, like imagination, was purely retentive. You may recall that Plato needed to conjecture a pre-existence for the soul in order to explain innate ideas. For Augustine, apparently innate ideas are the result of the ever-present contact between the soul and God. He was the first to use the term *internal sense* (*interior sensus*) in a roughly equivalent manner to Aristotle's common sense and he equates it with consciousness.[36]

Although Augustine is sometimes said to have discovered the inner life,[37] his influence on modern thought was in many ways less significant than that of the later Arabic thinkers who had better access to the works of Aristotle and whose philosophical views were less dominated by theology, despite their intense religiosity. But it was Augustine who most forcefully contributed the one big thing that has puzzled us and become a problem for us ever since. Therefore, his influence has extended far beyond Roman

Catholicism to Protestantism and to more secular thinkers such as Karl Jaspers and Hannah Arendt. Indeed, he is an inspiration for all who are fascinated and perplexed by human consciousness.

HOW THE MEDIEVAL ARABIC THINKERS MODIFIED THE ANCIENT WORLDVIEW

Islam, from its very inception, took a peculiar interest in human consciousness. But given its extreme God-centered orientation, this often took the form of attributing all knowledge or consciousness to God. The *Koran* retells the story in *Genesis* in which God bids Adam to name all of the animals. But in the Koranic version, it is God who supplies Adam with the correct names.[38] The Sufis are well known for their belief regarding all subjectivity or consciousness being a part of the divine Being. While this may appear similar to Hindu philosophical beliefs, Moslem thinkers were generally more careful to repudiate pantheism of the more objective variety.

Al-Ghazali, the great Persian thinker strongly influenced by Sufism, brought many of those ideas into the mainstream of Moslem and Arabic culture. While he was influential primarily in Sunni circles, similar ideas had already established themselves among the Shiites.[39] While al-Ghazali was an opponent of many of the Arabic philosophers we are about to discuss, the themes characteristic of his thought were somewhat pervasive in the Moslem world. Hence it may be a mistake to attribute this interest in consciousness to Neoplatonic philosophy alone. Nevertheless, he did appropriate many of the Neoplatonic metaphysical ideas of the very philosophers whom he opposed. Perhaps most interesting, for our purposes, is his notion of God as the light of heaven and earth.[40]

If one were to make a general (and therefore somewhat inaccurate) statement, the medieval Moslem thinkers took a greater interest in the human mind than in the external world, viewing it as closer to God. This is particularly true in thinkers like al-Ghazali, who did not believe in secondary causes or laws of nature. But it is also true of those Moslem and Arabic philosophers who did believe in an objectively determined universe. The ultimate result—a failure to take the objective pole of reality seriously—diminishes the separate reality of human existence as well, and there is a tendency in Islamic thought to subsume the soul in the overwhelming reality of God. Later on, Thomas Aquinas would oppose some of the views of Averroes by referring to the independent human will as proof of the separate reality of the human soul.

Medieval Arabic culture had a number of distinct advantages over Christendom prior to the thirteenth century. It was in much better touch with the ancient Greek philosophical texts. It resided in the area of the former Roman and Hellenistic Empires as well as in the birthplace of Judaism and Christianity. It had access to the glories of Persian and Hindu civilizations. In comparison, Christendom was uncultured and barbaric. But aside from its higher cultural level, what is of particular importance for us is the interest that the Arabic speaking philosophers (both Moslem and Jewish) took in Aristotle's *De Anima*.

When we look at those thinkers, who were responsible for re-acquainting the West with Aristotle, we find a tendency to conflate common sense and imagination and to place a much stronger emphasis on what was called the inner senses. Perhaps this is a reversion to a more generalized Semitic view of the inner person, as we saw earlier in the Hebrew Bible. Hence we find such thinkers as Alfarabi, Avicenna, Averroes, and Maimonides (an Arabic speaking Jew) merging the faculties of imagination, common sense, memory, and estimation. What all those faculties had in common from an Aristotelian perspective is that they are relatively low-level cognitive faculties, to be distinguished from pure perception on the one hand and pure reason on the other. In modern terminology, some of them are experiential while others are ideational. While the Arab philosophers continued to distinguish between reason and imagination, the fine distinctions that Aristotle had made were obliterated in favor of a more generalized concept of experience or consciousness. Albertus Magnus, Thomas Aquinas, Roger Bacon, and others relied heavily upon those Arabic sources in their discussions of the internal senses.[41]

It is interesting to relate this change to the consciousness of average human beings. Most people are neither careful observers, of nature, nor philosophers. The faculties that they tend to employ are often despised by philosophers and scientists as bastardized versions of true thought and perception and held to blame for the illusions of everyday life. But with the advent of the religions of revelation (Judaism, Christianity, and Islam), those seemingly inferior faculties took on a much greater significance. The interest in and search for the inner self (comprised of both experiences and ideas) was connected to a certain extent with religious and mystical experience. It set the stage for the stark contrast that we find in Cartesian thought between mind (consciousness) and matter. The psychological investigations of the Arabic Aristotelians found their way into Scholastic thought and then into modern thought. That emphasis on experience was significant in the Middle Ages as a major source of religious certainty.[42]

We in the modern world are so inured to changes in consciousness, whether they be the results of television, drugs, high speed travel, audio technology, amusement parks, etc., that it is difficult for us to imagine what a revolutionary change, that experientially based certainty, was. When a peasant left the countryside and entered a gothic cathedral he or she must have experienced an intensely altered state of consciousness. The same can surely be said of anyone who participates in Sufi rites. Perhaps a similarly powerful alteration of consciousness occurred in the ancient Jewish temple when simple people came from far and wide, believing that the very presence of God filled the Holy of Holies allowing for a vicarious expiation of sins. Needless to say, all religious rituals allow for the possibility of alterations of consciousness and such experiences by themselves really prove very little. The ancient Greek temples were indeed believed to be, and were experienced as, the abodes of specific gods. Undoubtedly, Dionysians, Pythagoreans, and other sects in the ancient Greco-Roman world favored extreme alterations in consciousness.[43]

Nevertheless, the normative religions that today dominate the West and the Islamic world (at least in some of their stages) allow for a much more radical transformation of consciousness than did the correlative normative religions of ancient Greece and Rome. Those ancient religions reflected normal superficial human concerns and were never taken very seriously by philosophers while the religions of revelation seem to plumb the very depths of human consciousness and were taken very seriously indeed by the great thinkers.[44] This should also be obvious from the religiously inspired art of both Christianity and Islam. Another comparison would be between the sculptures of the ancient world and those of the Italian Renaissance, which were modeled after them. Undoubtedly the ancient Greeks mastered the technical aspect of sculpture as far as is humanly possible and little or no improvement could be made upon it. But there is a quality of interiority in the Renaissance sculptures that the ancient ones simply don't possess.[45] Perhaps the greatest example of that experiential interiority, however, is the Gothic cathedral. That style of architecture emerged at a time in which Plato (particularly the *Timaeus*) and Aristotle were being rediscovered in Europe. The Gothic cathedral integrated otherworldly concerns, religious emotions, and aesthetic experience based upon light and the logic of physical space.

Any experiences that conflicted with official dogma could be labeled heretical in the Middle Ages. Nevertheless, in comparison with the ancient world, a much greater degree of individual experience was considered normal and valid. This sometimes led to the condemnation of various *kinds* of experience regardless of their content. The very fact that such experiences were condemned indicates their prevalence—in contrast to the ancient world, where only beliefs and actions tended to be condemned. For example, the only substantive charge brought against Socrates was that he taught others to reject the official gods: a charge that was probably false. His method of teaching, which both stemmed from and led to self-awareness and critical thinking, was far more dangerous but was hardly noticed at all. In the Middle Ages, Socrates was often viewed (by philosophical Jews, Christians, and Moslems) as a precursor of the true prophets rather than as a destroyer of human piety. That is because those religions (at least in their philosophical strands) reject the security of mythological thinking and stress instead the inner awareness of the solitary human being, whether he or she is a prophet or a philosopher.[46] Humankind was now fully aware of phenomenal consciousness but it was left to Descartes to clarify that awareness.

POST-MEDIEVAL VIEWS

Modernity is not a particularly clear and distinct concept. Certain events such as the adoption of Christianity and the fall of the Western Roman Empire mark the beginning of the medieval period. In contrast, there is no set of events that mark off the beginning of the modern age. Indeed, the kind of radical questioning of traditional beliefs that we associate with modernity had antecedents in Arabic, Jewish, and Christian thought in the Middle Ages. Perhaps the most significant changes, however, were the rise of modern science and the emergence of the nation state. This transfer of loyalty from tribe, religion, or class, and their concomitant myths and rituals, to something approaching universality, marks a major innovation in human evolution. In the Middle Ages, knowledge of Latin or Arabic allowed for a spirit of universality but perhaps only among intellectuals.[47] The nation state unites disparate classes, ethnicities and even religions in a striving towards a common destiny, and technology (the visible sign of modern science) does the same thing. And the very heterogeneity of our communal structures (in comparison to the clan or *polis* for example) allows for a much greater wealth of individual experience. This is the culmination of trends clearly observable in the Middle Ages just as the thought of Descartes is the culmination of trends in medieval philosophy.

THE RENAISSANCE

Without taking a position on the relative uniqueness of Renaissance thought, it certainly does appear to me that the modern world has benefited greatly from the discussions that took place within that rather short historical period. This has not always been fully appreciated by those who view modern science as the *sine qua non* of modernity. But if we take another position and view the essence of modernity as the rise of individuality and freedom, then the Renaissance takes on an extreme importance. Paul Oscar Kristeller, perhaps our greatest expert on the Renaissance, noted this supposed conflict between scientific thought and uniquely human problems.[48] Actually it is only a conflict in some small minds. But if my thesis is correct and consciousness can only be understood within a truly human context, Renaissance thought may be of particular interest to us.

Often we tend to view Renaissance thinking as a rehashing of ancient Greek culture but nothing could be further from the truth. The Renaissance was at least as dependent upon Augustine, the Arabic philosophers and Aquinas as it was on ancient Greece. This should become apparent from a short sketch of the thought of Ficino and Pico. What comes across in those thinkers is a new or at least unabashed reliance upon the self, along with a willingness to explore a multitude of historical sources. This sets the stage for the revolution in human thought that we associate with such rationalist thinkers as Descartes and Spinoza.

Ficino was without a doubt the greatest of Renaissance thinkers. Since this is not the place for a full exposition of his thought we will confine ourselves to those issues that bear directly upon consciousness. Ficino took a special interest in those Neoplatonic writers such as Plotinus and Iamblichus who dealt with the ascent of the soul to a divine realm. In accordance with Neoplatonic views that will be looked at more closely in subsequent chapters, Ficino believed that above the soul is an incorporeal mind that is the home of the angels. Although animals have souls (*anima*) only humans have a rational soul (*animus*).

Without going into great detail,[49] it is worthwhile to contrast this view with some other ways of thinking. Unlike in Plato's teaching, the soul now reports to a mind and not a form. This may seem quite similar to Philo and the Neoplatonists but it is also combined with an intense Augustinian interest in the inner life. That great curiosity had perhaps been blunted by the great synthesis achieved by Albert the Great and Aquinas. Ficino studied Greek, which was a relatively new phenomenon among scholars. Neither the Scholastics nor the Arabic philosophers had direct access to Greek. His *Platonic Theology* was designed to show that Greek philosophy proves the immortality of the soul and its ability to perceive even in its earthly life the permeating presence of God in the soul and in the world. This re-emphasis on the immortality of the soul is somewhat unique and came before the doctrine became an official dogma of the Roman Catholic Church in 1513 with the Lateran Council. What is unique about it is the combining of an insistence on immortality with a vigorous belief in the dignity of the individual. This may be an intuition that we have still not fully accepted. (For reasons that we can not go into in depth, the doctrine of immortality has often been used by groups who actually oppose the dignity of the individual. And this has engendered a counter reaction from those who do). In addition, Ficino, like Aquinas before him, set out to show that the doctrine of Averroes regarding the Active Intellect is false and that immortality pertains to the individual soul.[50] But unlike Aquinas', Ficino's motives were not primarily theological but perhaps philosophical in a more practical sense; he aimed to assist and inspire individuals in their own contemplative enterprises.

Giovanni Pico della Mirandola, whose creative life was cut short by an early death, distinguished himself by his willingness to explore varied avenues of human thought. His interest in Arabic and Hebrew set the stage for a Western civilization that today is truly interested in all human cultural phenomena. But unlike some of our current eclectic interests, Pico's investigations were motivated by a firm conception of the essential nature of humankind, or perhaps we should say the lack of any such essential nature. This notion of an exalted humanity related to God and superior to all natural phenomena sets the stage for the explosion of human freedom in the modern world. His *Oration on Human Dignity* is perhaps the Renaissance work that most closely anticipates modernity, although we can not expect to find a truly modern person in the Renaissance. For example, scholars continue to debate as to whether Pico was really interested in exotic belief systems or only used them to further his own theological agenda. Nevertheless, his erudition was enormous considering his age and the fact that he never really had the chance to fully mature.

Pico was obsessed with the notion of divinely authorized human power: something that would later be communicated to Descartes in a dream. Pico's notion that humanity has no fixed form or essence allows for a previously unimagined freedom to pursue understanding and/or salvation but also earthly power, as long as it recognizes the ultimate authority of God. This combining of theoretical and practical interests is somewhat of a break from the ancient and medieval worlds, and it ushers in modernity's obsession with practicality. But perhaps an even better example of this Renaissance ideal is Leonardo da Vinci.

The thought of Leonardo was a product of the Italian Renaissance but was also quite idiosyncratic. In his notebooks he discusses the role of the senses, reason, common sense, memory, and imagination in the acquisition of knowledge. You will recall that for both the ancients and the medieval thinkers, knowledge is acquired by relying upon certain faculties and disregarding others; in a sense, it was considered a gift of the gods. What is unique in Leonardo's thought is the strong emphasis on perception as a vehicle for obtaining knowledge of the world, but one that differs radically from the empiricist school that we are so influenced by today. It is for that reason that his drawings have always and will always fascinate us; they display a view of the world that is quite akin to ours yet includes so much more. A recent exhibit of his drawings at the Metropolitan Museum of Art, for example, set an all-time record for viewers.

Like the ancient Greeks, Leonardo believed that mathematical relationships were crucial in both science and art. But in other respects Leonardo's concept of beauty varied quite a bit from that of the ancient Greeks. Indeed, for Leonardo (unlike the ancients), science and technology were inseparable just as science and art were inseparable. Art, particularly painting, reveals the inner reality of the world that science explains in terms of mathematical models. The real test of those models, however, is technological progress. The genius of Leonardo points out as nothing else can the immaturity of the ancients, who were as incapable of truly original art as they were of technological innovation, despite their highly developed faculties of rational thought and aesthetic appreciation. For Leonardo, the acquisition of knowledge involved not only the senses and theoretical reason but also involved the *sensus communis*, memory, imagination, and judgment.

Another interesting feature of Leonardo's thought is his insistence upon the superiority of painting to any of the other arts. This was a radical approach since painting seemed more dependent upon the inferior and individual faculty of imagination than sculpture and less dependent upon abstract thought than architecture, poetry and prose. This view placed the individual and his/her imagination squarely in the center of the acquisition of knowledge. His appreciation of the feminine is also remarkable, especially considering his unusual sexuality.[51]

MODERNITY

Descartes is often called the first modern philosopher. Where one draws these lines is somewhat arbitrary, as I will illustrate more fully in a later chapter. In some respects his thought was quite similar to the medieval and Renaissance thinkers. But in at least one area he made a major breakthrough even though he has been vilified for it in recent years. There is a sense in which we are all Cartesians now, just as none of us are really Aristotelians, and this is true even when we deny the very distinctions that Descartes insisted upon. This is an indication of how decisively he has influenced our thinking and for that reason he does indeed deserve that aforementioned title.

What is especially significant in Cartesian thought is that the major distinctions are no longer between the various mental faculties and their relationship to substantial objective reality, as was so typical of medieval thought. The big distinction that has bedeviled Western thought ever since Descartes is between mind (consciousness) and matter or between individual subjectivity and impersonal objective reality. We find in his writings a tendency to reduce the many internal senses to one and to contrast that with the external senses.[52] Hence it appears that the influence of Augustine, the Medieval, might have been exercised most powerfully through Descartes, the first modern philosopher. This will be explored more deeply in a subsequent chapter (Although

Descartes was the early modern thinker who most carefully distinguished mind from matter, that general trend can also be observed in a much wider circle of thinkers).

Another example of this modern sensibility can be found once again in the perception of the beautiful and the sublime.[53] Let us look at the thinker whose views mark the transition from classicism to romanticism in the English-speaking world: Edmund Burke. His notion of beauty or sublimity contained elements that would have made the ancient Greeks cringe: terror, weakness, pain, and delicacy. These qualities, far from confirming us in the conviction that we humans are the measure of all things, instill in us feelings of astonishment and inadequacy. Feelings like that help provoke in us the deep inwardness so characteristic of modernity. In other words, consciousness is intensified when the harmonious relationship between the human being and his or her environment is disturbed. For Burke, it is the infinite with its inherent lack of clarity and distinctness that produces the greatest beauty. And those large or powerful things that fill us with an experience of the sublime do so precisely by making us feel overwhelmed and inadequate. Therefore, the female, associated with weakness, is the more beautiful gender.[54] Where the sublime begins, action ends, and the connections between form and function, so precious to the ancient Greeks, are severed.[55]

So we seem to have come full circle to the notion of soul as knowledge or perception (consciousness) and emphatically not as originator of movement. This notion of consciousness, however, is now somewhat divorced from external physical reality. You might recall that for the ancient Greeks it was just the opposite: those who viewed soul as consciousness (perception and knowledge) tended to identify it with the forces of nature. Plato's great innovation was to liken it instead to the eternal Forms, which while not forces of nature were still objective entities. In other words, for the ancients, human consciousness was simply a reflection of objective reality with no inherent freedom. Freedom and individuality, if they existed at all, could only be found in private practical activity. For modernity, on the other hand, the perceiving and conceptualizing of objective reality is also an arena of freedom. This becomes especially evident in the use modern people make of their mental energies. It results in such public events as economic striving, technology, capitalism, social revolutions, etc.

In a world that has been disenchanted and deprived of psychic energy, the human mind becomes the sole locus of creative causality. This becomes quite evident (sometimes painfully so) in post-impressionist art. On the one hand, its non-representational aspect can be viewed as insuring its genuine creativity (see Danto, 1964). But on the other hand, more recent attempts to enshrine replicas of everyday material objects as art makes an even bolder statement. It seems to assert the ultimate ability of individual creativity to transcend everything (even the most mundane and practical articles of consumer culture). As Arthur Danto ends his famous article "The Artworld": "Brillo boxes may reveal us to ourselves as well as anything might: a mirror held up to nature, they might serve to catch the conscience of our kings."(Danto, 1964, 584). Individual human consciousness seems to have emerged absolutely triumphant, but the reader will perhaps forgive my rhetorical question. Does this victory really warrant celebration?[56]

CONCLUSION
Ancient thought, like so-called primitive thought, does not make a strong distinction between subjectivity and objectivity. The emergence of monotheistic religions centered subjectivity in God and humanity and left the remainder of objective reality disenchanted. Secularization and the growth of science accelerated that disenchantment of the world. Consciousness is now viewed as a completely separate phenomenon and one that might be an illusion unless it can be shown to link up with objective reality.

Despite our intense intuition that consciousness is *sui generis*, however, we retain the need to integrate it with our knowledge of everything else because the latter constitutes reality for us. Hence arises the consciousness problem. In addition, there will always remain the primordial human desire to re-enchant the world. If we were able to take the final step of completely divorcing consciousness from the objective realm of being, there would be no such problem. And since most of us can not or will not do that (or return to the views of the ancients), the problem remains and it may never be definitively resolved. Yet in all great art and particularly in certain kinds of art, we can obtain a glimpse of that elusive connection or unity between human subjectivity and the objective physical world.

Some extreme types of modern art purport to have no representational content and simply mirror sensations or express feelings, or they mock objective reality by reproducing its most uninspiring aspects. This expresses hyperbolically our modern concept of individual consciousness as *sui generis* and glorifies human subjectivity above objective reality (and even its supposed Creator). Most art, however, has continued to combine representational content with subjective experience, although the latter came to be emphasized more and more as the hold of classicism on Western art loosened. The ancient Greeks would not have recognized that their concept of the beautiful was somewhat subjective nor would some medieval artists have recognized the subjective nature of their intensely religious themes. A deep blending of the objective and subjective occurred in romantic art. Classical art stressed the objective but was later found to be cold and distant, with the exception of those great masters who were able to transcend their genre. Modern art tends towards the subjective, allowing each spectator to create his or her own experience, but when it goes too far in that direction questions are raised regarding its value. This may also illustrate the aesthetic intuition that objectivity and subjectivity emerge out of the same ultimate reality. Each person, however, must decide for herself or himself to what extent such intuitions are to be trusted.

NOTES

1. See Levinson, 2003, 99–105 for a good discussion. Aesthetic experience, like all experience, can be viewed as phenomenal or epistemic. In either case, it is characterized as intense, complex and unified and the latter characteristic sets it apart from some other types of experience.

2. This might initially be viewed as evidence for dualism. As has often been noted, every work of art can be described both physically and aesthetically,

and it seems impossible to profitably reduce one to the other. In fact, the more *crucial* qualities (from the aesthetic perspective) are not physical. Some have attempted to conceptualize this relationship as one of embodiment. See Margolis (1974), "Works of Art . . .". This concept, of course, also smacks of dualism. But it does not take much investigation to determine that works of art not only are physical but also are the creations of physical beings working with physical media, etc. Therefore, such a limited but persuasive investigation seems to militate in favor of neutral monism. That monism could take various forms but one that is primarily physical and conceives of consciousness as a mere emergent quality would seem to violate the primacy of the aesthetic perspective, for which experience is crucial. This will be discussed shortly. I will also argue that experience is crucial for our notion of a human person even if we are willing to admit as humans those who cannot experience anything such as persons in persistent vegetative states.

3. *Journal of Consciousness Studies*, 8, 9–10: 48.

4. See Wilkes, 1964. This is an attractive proposition for those who would like to deny phenomenal consciousness. If you can show that a rational, sophisticated culture can get along just fine without such a concept, it takes you quite a way toward your goal. But, interestingly, the point has also been made by some who believe in phenomenal consciousness. For example, Hamlyn sees in Aristotle's failure to note a mind-body problem an inadequacy in the Aristotelian concept of the soul. See D W Hamlyn, 1968, xiii.

5. Panpsychism is often associated with *primitive* thought and some people are quick to disavow it, but David Chalmers, a very modern scholar, espouses it, as do many others.

6. One must distinguish between two distinct yet related current meanings of *aesthetic*, both related to its etymology. The concept of beauty is not confined to art since both nature and mathematics are beautiful. And art need not be beautiful, as much modern art proves. Nevertheless, the term *aesthetics* has come to mean the philosophy of art (though in a broader sense it can mean the philosophy of beauty). In general, art must be experienced in the limited sense of being perceived. But that is not strictly true of literature. Nevertheless, even literature, in contrast to merely factual reporting, must have a "feel" to it. Therefore, one must not attempt to confine experience or consciousness to perception or sensation. This will be discussed more fully in later chapters.

7. See Gregory, 1987, 8.

8. I will not take a position on the question regarding whether what one experiences in art is the expression of the artist's feelings, one's own experiences, or a cultural context. The most common-sensical answer includes

all three. But perhaps it can be asserted that at least one of the first two, and the relative of the third, is more characteristic of modern art.

9. There is some room for debate regarding this assertion. As is well known, Dilthey argued that the world of nature is essentially foreign to humankind, in contrast to society or culture, where he or she feels at home. "Nature is alien to us. . . . Society is our world." (Dilthey, 1989, 88). This leads to the conclusion that we can never really understand nature the way we understand human reality and therefore can never really feel certainty regarding physical scientific knowledge. Popper denied the validity of that distinction and asserted that physical scientists may indeed experience that same feeling of certainty. Yet his whole system of falsification seems to question that contention. Medieval or Renaissance art can never be falsified, as were their respective sciences; they remain as valid as ever. I also think it is fair to say that *most* people do not experience the deep certainty and satisfaction with science that they do with religion, art, or politics. Nevertheless, as Dr. Nassir Ghaemi has reminded me in a personal communication, there are many for whom science is a religion.

10. For a fairly exhaustive treatment, see MacDonald, 2003, 2–12. In addition to those he mentions, there are also other Hebrew nouns (many of which denote parts of the body) that function in the Bible as descriptions of the inner person. Some examples are *ayin* (eye), *kebod* (liver), *kilyah* (kidneys), *etzem* (bone). There are two other major contenders for soul (*ruach* and *neshama*), both of which denote wind or breath and are often described as coming from God.

11. Our post-Cartesian view of the soul sees it as the seat of thought, consciousness and will. There are a number of passages in the Bible where *nephesh* appears to mean will (e.g., Jeremiah 15:1, Genesis 23:8, Deuteronomy 21:14). A close inspection, however, reveals that these particular usages may really refer to inclination or desire.

12. There have been a number of attempts to contrast the Greek (occidental) mind with the Hebrew (oriental), e.g. Mathew Arnold. It is of interest that Buber considered the former to be more inward; see Buber, 1972, 39–41. That is obviously not the view of this author. One of the problems is the extensive influence that the two cultures have exerted upon one another. Some cognitive motifs that we consider Greek are actually oriental and vice versa.

13. For a most exhaustive treatment, see MacDonald, 2003, 12–35.

14. MacDonald dismisses it and explains away the phenomenon of the *double* as something unrelated to immortality. Although this is not my area of expertise, I am somewhat skeptical regarding these discussions whether regarding Greek or Hebrew thought. The writers of the ancient Greek and Hebrew narratives may well have not believed in immortality but folk

traditions found room for such a belief. We cannot conclude that belief in life after bodily death is an invention of Pythagoras, Plato, the Pharisees, etc.

15. See Plato, *The Phaedo*, 100. Plato's view of the soul is actually quite complicated and I use *The Phaedo* only as an example of a lack of interest in subjectivity. For a more exhaustive account, see MacDonald, 2003, 37–54.

16. See Plato, *Timaeus*, 44b.

17. See ibid., 91e–92a

18. See Aristotle, *De Anima*, 404a–405b.

19. Another possibility is that Aristotle viewed himself as a Platonist and simply took it for granted that all Platonists agree with Anaxagoras. For good arguments for viewing Aristotle as a Platonist, see Gerson, 2005. As a matter of fact, both Plato and Aristotle tend to view the human soul and God as Forms (or as related to them).

20. See Plato, *The Phaedo*, 98.

21. Aristotle, *De Anima*, 404b.

22. We can speak of unconscious perception or knowledge in animals, humans, and even machines.

23. This may appear to be an astounding observation and one that we rarely acknowledge. While we may use similar classifications of the human psyche as Aristotle did, the significance that we give the categories is quite different. For him, the significant dichotomy is form and matter, while for us it is subjectivity and objectivity.

24. Aristotle, *De Anima*, III.3. 427b, 11–16.

25. Burnyeat, 1992, 26.

26. As Herbert Read stated regarding the artist: "We expect him to reveal something to us that is original—a unique and private vision of the world." See Read, 1951, 33. I have bypassed the debate regarding whether works of art can be expressive. There is a school of analytical philosophy that denies that romantic notion. Personally, I find Popper's notions of World 2 and World 3 to be good ways of conceptualizing the connection between culture and human consciousness. See Popper, (1994). For a good critical discussion of expressivity in art, see Sircello, 1978.

27. The paradigm is physical toil for subsistence but any kind of specialized effort contributes to one-sidedness and is opposed to the Greek concept of virtue as moderation. See Buckhardt, 1998, 185–86.

28. Perhaps Arthur Danto stated it best. "Socrates saw mirrors as but reflecting what we can already see; so art, insofar as mirror-like, yields idle accurate duplications of the appearance of things, and is of no cognitive benefit whatever. Hamlet, more accurately, recognized a remarkable feature of reflecting surfaces, namely that they show us what we could not otherwise perceive—our own face and form" (Danto, 1964, 571). Nevertheless,

ancient Greek art, despite the ideal, was much more than mere imitation and/or geometrical perfection. Ancient Greek vases are the paradigm of that perfection, which (according to Herbert Read) renders them "cold and life-less" (Read, 1951, 28). But, as Read readily admits, Greek sculpture often "distorted in the interest of the ideal" (Ibid., 29). This illustrates a necessary truth about human behavior. If something exists within the human being (such as freedom, individuality, or phenomenal consciousness) it will some-how find its expression, even in a culture that denies its reality.

29. Plato, *The Republic*, Book X, 598.

30. See Plato, *Hippias Major*.

31. For that reason biblical anthropomorphism can never be completely eliminated. If you had a god that only calculated but did not feel, regret, or communicate, it would appear to be more like a computer and not at all like a person. The unique insight of the Bible is that personhood *is* the ultimate reality. Eventually we may understand that God's personhood is quite dif-ferent from ours, but we come to that understanding gradually and imper-fectly. We can never really separate this belief from the only personhood with which we are directly acquainted.

32. See Plotinus, *The Enneads*, 1.2.5.1–26.

33. See *Quod Animi Mores* in Galen, *Scripta Minora*, 2.67.2 16.

34. See his commentary on *De Anima*, 25.4–9.

35. It has often been claimed that psychological disruption and trauma intensifies human self-awareness or interest in the inner life. Jaspers (1954, 20), views suffering or forsakenness as one pillar of philosophy.

36. See Augustine, *The Confessions*, I, 20, VII, 17, and *De Libero Arbitrio*, II, 3–5.

37. See Jaspers, *Plato and Augustine,* (1957), 71: "Never before had a man faced his soul in this way." Menn, 1998, 23, states that Ambrose and Augustine were the first Latin Christian thinkers to maintain that the human soul is incorporeal. These two claims are related. We have seen that many ancient thinkers did not draw a firm line between subjectivity and objectivity, but instead viewed the soul as a formal reality and therefore still related to material reality. The notion of extreme incorporeality, which re-emerges in Descartes, implies something strange and invites curiosity. Or perhaps the introspection is the cause of the new philosophical perspec-tive on the soul.

38. See in the Koran, *al Baqara*, 2:30. This story regarding God, Adam, and the angels may have its origins in a rabbinic *midrash*.

39. See Henry Corbin's article in *The Encyclopedia of Philosophy*, 1967, 327–28.

40. For a fuller discussion, see Majid Fakhry's *History of Islamic Philoso-phy*, 1983, 246–50.

41. For a fuller discussion of the internal senses in Arabic, Scholastic and early modern philosophers see Wolfson, 1977, 250–314.

42. It is not always fully appreciated how mystical many of the medieval Arabic philosophers really were. This is evident in the interplay between Sufism and philosophy in such figures as ibn Tufayl, an associate of Averroes and Abraham Maimonides, the son of Moses Maimonides. Conversely, as we have seen, an ostensibly anti-philosophical Arabic thinker, al-Ghazali, was actually quite sophisticated philosophically. His suspicion regarding the power of matter and secondary causes pre-figures the arguments of Descartes and the occasionalists.

43. The Greek *polis* was suspicious of individual consciousness. It is perhaps for that reason that the infectious mob cult of Dionysus became so incredibly popular in Greece, and Pythagoras, with a greater emphasis on the individual, moved his cult to southern Italy. See Burckhardt, 1998, 211–13 for a good discussion.

44. The reason for this might be found in the relationship between the ancient Greeks and their gods. It was not a particularly loving relationship. Zeus, as is well known, denied fire and other useful technologies to humanity (to whom the gods of Greek mythology are related and competing beings). Consequently, Greek religious thought and experience tends to be impersonal, something that it shares with eastern thought. This contrasts greatly with biblical or Abrahamic religions despite the fact that remnants of a similar mythological rivalry between humanity and God can be found in the Bible. Human consciousness, while requiring a certain amount of rationality, is intensified by love and what is sometimes called the I-Thou relationship. Perhaps that is why hearing, the sense most related to love, is accorded such great importance in biblical literature. This contrasts with both ancient and modern rationalism for which sight is the most important sense.

45. I will admit that the relative absence of original ancient Greek sculpture (in contrast to Roman imitations) makes this assertion somewhat shaky.

46. This conflation of the roles of prophet and philosopher is seen most clearly in al Farabi, who thought that either a prophet or a philosopher could found a virtuous state, and in Maimonides who (wrongly) believed that a prophet must be a philosopher.

47. The restriction to intellectuals was more marked in the Christian world because of the proliferation of vernaculars. In the Muslim world, on the other hand, one language (Arabic) pervaded the entire empire (with certain exceptions). Nevertheless, because of the existence of various dialects and levels of prestige among various types of Arabic, the situations were not altogether dissimilar.

48. See Kristeller, 1979, 168.

49. For a fuller account see MacDonald, 2003, 217–34.

50. Averroes is an example of the denial of individual immortality combined with defense of the intellectual dignity of the individual. The Active
Intellect was first mentioned somewhat obliquely by Aristotle. Some later
com-mentators considered it as outside of the human intellect, which was
conceived as passive. The active intellect was conceived by some medievals
as the lowest of the separate intelligences or angels. It was responsible for
the ability of human beings to think. Therefore, for some medieval thinkers,
the human soul was relatively unimportant in comparison with other creations or emanations from God. But for others the Active Intellect was
much more exalted: either God or the *Logos*. Averroes believed not only
that it was outside of the human intellect but that even all passive human
intellects were ultimately one in the Active Intellect. Hence individual
immortality is a myth. Later thinkers, such as Pompanazzi, attempted to reconcile this belief with Catholic dogma by a kind of double truth theory:
immortality is assured by faith and revelation, even as it is rejected by reason.

51. Leonardo has often been described as basically homosexual and/or asex-
ual. Yet "Leonardo was extremely sensitive to the beauty of the female
body; one could even say that he was the first to realize the soft texture of
the skin" (Wolfflin, 1966, 54).

52. See Descartes, *The Meditations*, II (oeuvres, ed. Adam et Tannery, I,
p.263, 11. 6–8), where he identifies imagination and common sense, and
contrasts them with the external senses. This would explain why, for Descartes, animals can sense stimuli but are not conscious.

53. I will not attempt to distinguish the beautiful from the sublime as some
philosophers have done, as it is not relevant to my purpose.

54. Although I am not prepared to argue the point convincingly, it is interesting to contrast this perception with that of the ancient Greeks who had
somewhat different views regarding human beauty.

55. See Burke (1757). To what extent Burke's aesthetic theory coheres with
his social and political beliefs is a provocative question. Dr. Nassir Ghaemi
(in a personal communication) argued that his negative view of human
nature prompted his conservative political views, some of which are akin to
those found in the U.S. Constitution. It seems to me that there is a biblical
insight, which Burke shared, that there is something fundamentally wrong
with humankind. Therefore, human cleverness will confound any well-
thought-out social system and humankind can never rest in a harmonious
superiority to the rest of creation. This insight sets Burke apart from the
classical political thinkers (including Aristotle), all of whom thought that
politics was subservient to reason and virtue. Nevertheless, political systems (according to Burke) are necessary, and function best when they con-
form to tradition. Hence it would appear that both his aesthetic and political

views are reactions against abstract rationalistic philosophies of the human person.

56. There is a traditional view that in order to qualify as art an object must be an artifact, which is to say it must be man-made. So Duchamp's urinal, re-named "Fountain" can be a work of art but a beautiful piece of driftwood cannot. Perhaps this traditional distinction rested upon an understandable reluctance to take credit for what the ultimate Creator has wrought. But even this inhibition has been questioned by Jack Glickman and others. In 1976 he thought that pieces of driftwood were still not "universally" considered as art but argued that "there is no conceptual absurdity in the idea of a work of art created by someone but made by no one." See Glickman, 1978, 157. I am not sure whether this inhibition is still generally upheld or whether we have moved to Glickman's position. At any rate, it is quite likely that future generations will no longer make that distinction.

Chapter Three

Consciousness and Creative Causality

Causality is a critical feature of the mysterious relationship between mind and matter. In fact many people deny the ultimate distinction between mind and matter precisely because there is no adequate way to conceptualize their causal interaction. This leads many to physicalism and others to neutral monism. I will now attempt to show that reflection upon how causality (in the broad sense) might operate in the incipient stages of creation, prior to the existence of the physical world (as we know it) led many towards idealist positions in metaphysics.

There seems to be a rather prevalent and I think mistaken notion in the consciousness literature regarding consciousness and causality. That mistake is to conflate the efficient cause of consciousness with its true nature, and it can be found in both physicalist and functionalist thinkers. The former focus on the immediate causes of consciousness (neuron firings). The latter focus on the dynamic interaction between an organism (or machine) and its environment that would have allowed for consciousness to obtain an ecological foothold. In both cases prior efficient causes are viewed as the key to an understanding of the nature of consciousness. This may perhaps be a holdover from the ancient and medieval notion that a cause is always superior to its effect.[1] It derives from Aristotle's assertion that in order to truly know what something is one must know its causes, which will also reveal why it is.[2] Spinoza also accepted that proposition but the causality that concerned him was mainly efficient causality. Aristotle was concerned not only with efficient causality but with material, formal, and final causes as well. When those are narrowed down to efficient causality, knowledge of causes no longer yields such understanding. Hence Damasio's attempt to understand spiritual yearnings in terms of actual experiences of suffering and death in the process of human evolution simply does not work.[3] I will argue that the hard problem of consciousness is not a problem of efficient causality at all and answers to such causal questions do not help much in determining the true nature of consciousness. Therefore if my reasoning is correct, Damasio's ostensible argument for neutral monism is not a good one at all, but perhaps he has other less obvious reasons for embracing that doctrine. I will briefly examine panpsychism and neutral monism again and propose an alternative metaphysical view. Finally, I will attempt to show how those theories do contain important elements of truth that can be incorporated into the proposed alternative.

THE HARD PROBLEM

We have already discussed the consciousness problem, which is essentially a problem of conceptualizing the relationship between mind and matter. The so-called hard problem has been enunciated by David Chalmers who characterized it as follows: "Why is all this processing accompanied by an experienced inner life?"[4] It was expressed as follows by Keith Sutherland (referring to the work of Susan Greenfield): "how a subjective inner world is generated from a lump of neuronal sludge."[5] I am not sure if these are really the same problem. If I understand Chalmers correctly, the problem stems from the fact that everything else that we know about animal and even human life could conceivably go on quite well without that inner experience that we call consciousness and therefore consciousness seems unnecessary from an evolutionary standpoint. The problem indicated by Sutherland's and Greenfield's use of the term "neuronal sludge" seems to stem from the fact that consciousness is so utterly different from (and superior to) the physical correlates (the sludgy stuff) that we consider to be its efficient causes. My intuition, however, is that the questions are closely related. Useless physical organs like the appendix can be easily explained away despite the fact that they are not (in Owen Flanagan's terminology) "fitness enhancing,"[6] but the strangeness of consciousness in a physical world seems to require a different kind of explanation.[7] This may not be a "how does it happen" problem but a "why does it happen" or "how is it possible" question.[8] It is also more than an explanatory gap because such gaps exist all over the place without provoking hard problems.

Even if we were to have the causality established and had discovered invariant laws of nature that explain how neuron firings produce consciousness and even how consciousness was of sufficient survival value to carve out an ecological niche, some people would still suspect that there is something ontologically important here that we don't yet understand.[9] Therefore, Damasio's attempt to answer the question is not really effective. He asks: "Why do we need a 'mind level' of brain operations as opposed to a 'neural map level' alone...?" The answers he gives are as follows. "Even temporary suspensions of consciousness entail an inefficient management of life. . . . Even the mere suspension of the self-component of consciousness entails a disruption of life management and returns a human being to a state of dependence comparable to that of a toddler."[10] I am sure that he is correct about the facts but this begs the question. Presumably, creatures could have evolved with other *unconscious* mechanisms that were roughly equally efficient.[11] And that would have been a much simpler (and more probable) adaptation.

So far, the best answers that have come out of the consciousness literature (at least the literature that I have read) are panpsychism and neutral monism. The former may be a very primitive belief (which doesn't mean that it is false). It is characteristic of primitive people to see the physical world as populated by spirits and this is usually called animism.[12] Modern panpsychists, however, often tend towards idealism[13] and perhaps it would be useful to distinguish between those two views. David Chalmers, for example, admits to being a property dualist, considers his views to be a variant of panpsychism,[14] and suggests that there might even be natural laws that are not physical laws. I am in agreement with him that consciousness is as primitive a concept as matter, time, or space. Given that assumption, one might expect to find it everywhere. But is it everywhere?

Neutral monism is not quite so old as animism, but dates back at least as far as Spinoza. It asserts that reality is neither physical nor mental but is really neutral as regards that dichotomy. As we have seen previously, this is a very profound idea but it raises some difficult questions, some of which will be discussed in this and the next chapter. Assuming that the ultimate reality is neither mind nor matter, why does it bifurcate itself into mind and matter? It seems that we have no answer to this unless we postulate an additional reality akin to consciousness, will, or mind, or admit that all our beliefs about reality are delusions.

What is interesting about those two models is that they rest on unexamined metaphors that are exemplified by the saying "it goes all the way down." That saying certainly applies to panpsychism and I would suggest an analogous saying for monism: "it goes all the way out." Both metaphors (down and out) seem to refer to the physical world, as they are spatial metaphors. With panpsychism, one goes down to primitive forms of life and even non-living entities to find the origin of consciousness. With neutral monism, one goes out from one's perceptual field. If I am a monist and I see a tree, rather than believing that there is a physical tree and a mental sense datum, I say that the same ultimate reality lies behind both appearances. But what do I say about all the trees that I don't see? I would believe that they also are neither physical nor mental. But that implies continuity between what I perceive and what I don't perceive. Such a continuous world seems to be either a physical world (or at least a material world) or a vast mind because a reality that is neither mind nor matter would seem to have no properties at all, including the property of continuity. This is another example of the physicality bias that intuitively views being as physical and the origin of mind and consciousness in inanimate, unintelligent, physical matter. Hence, neutral monism in modern thought seems to be an offshoot of physicalism but one that allows consciousness in through the back door as long as it doesn't make too much noise.

A DIFFERENT APPROACH

I think that the view of the origin of mind and consciousness just enunciated has no logical basis whatsoever and is really a kind of mythology. I will grant, however, that this is a mythology generally favored by natural scientists perhaps for good psychological (but not logical) reasons. The job of natural science is to push naturalistic explanations to their limits, and therefore it recognizes no limits to them whatsoever. I take this to be a methodological principle and not an ontological one.[15] Panpsychism and neutral monism may appear to be continuations of that naturalistic research program but they are not, in my estimation, scientific theories. Not only do they not provide a basis for making new predictions, they don't seem to provide a simple or elegant rationale for the correlations between neuron firings and consciousness that we are already aware of and seek to explain. They are metaphysical theories that may or may not prove scientifically fruitful. Like most metaphysical views, they provide a kind of understanding of things but don't explain why things are the way they are, and not some other way. Nor is the alternative that I will propose a scientific theory. Therefore, nothing I will say should have any effect on scientific methodology, but it might affect the meta-scientific views of scientists or others.

When I speak of a mythology I mean a belief system that projects human qualities onto some other reality as a means of explaining human origins. Mythologies (in that broad sense) are not necessarily bad. A case could be made that they are essential to any deep conception of humanity. Therefore one should not confuse this meaning of mythology with the more restricted sense of a belief system that is plainly false. Plato's two worlds model is an example of a myth as is the biblical view of a creator God.

Neither of them is plainly false, self-evidently true, or deduced from empirical evidence. Just as the ancient Greeks projected lust and petty jealousy onto their gods in order to explain human origins, some of us project consciousness onto the physical world since we believe humanity evolved out of lower life forms and ultimately out of inanimate physical entities.[16] The metaphor "goes all the way down" is part of that mythology. I propose an alternative metaphor: consciousness goes all the way up! But before I do that I would like to point out why origin myths going back to inanimate matter—or lumps of sludge—are ultimately misguided.

Many people, myself included, wonder how consciousness could have arisen in a world without consciousness. Right or wrong, our intuition tells us that the effect cannot contain something that is totally lacking in the cause. This was an intuition that Spinoza shared. As I understand Descartes, efficient physical causality can't be the whole story and he also had the same intuition. While I don't completely trust that intuition, I also suspect that the very notion of a world without consciousness is incoherent. Perhaps you can't have a world without consciousness because, as Kant taught, the universe is not a thing but an idea (and a rather sophisticated one requiring conscious thought). Some would deny this, however, and argue that sophisticated thought processes can indeed be unconscious. Perhaps this is another example of the physicality bias.

Perceptions of physical things or sensations that derive from the physical senses are often considered the paradigms of consciousness while abstract thought processes often are not. But in reality both are sometimes conscious and sometimes not. People have non-experiential ideas that orient them in time and space just as they have non-experiential sensory awareness of the physical world. But it seems to me that anyone who can think *about* the universe has had experiences, just as anyone who has really listened to music has. You can brainwash people subliminally but such unconscious ideation is not the same as profound thought, which is itself an experience. I often wonder how people who think deeply about things or appreciate music and art can be materialists.

Perhaps their experiential level is low relative to their mental computational level and they don't notice what is right in front of them: phenomenal consciousness.

According to the view that I am proposing, the subject-object split is crucial not only to consciousness but also to the idea of a stable physical universe. It is not simply that consciousness is a chronic *feature* of the physical universe (as can be explained by neutral monism and panpsychism) but consciousness is a necessary *condition* for that universe (both for its creation and its cognition).[17] Those who have read the preface and introduction carefully will understand why this may sound suspiciously like religious notions that many consciousness investigators would be desirous of rejecting.[18] It is certainly not a model of efficient causality. But many philosophers and scientists who deal with problems of causality in quantum mechanics and social science have also argued for an expanded view of causality.

A MEDIEVAL MODEL

Some medieval thinkers favored an alternative model.[19] I suspect if you seriously consider it, you may agree that it is no less reasonable than the other two models and may even explain more. The fact that it may be antithetical to certain contemporary sensibilities ought not to disqualify it in the long run. The thinkers that I am referring to equated God's power to create with His self-knowledge (which, I take it, would be a form of consciousness) originating from Themistius' fourth century commentary on Book Lambda of the *Metaphysics*—translated into Arabic in the ninth century, Hebrew in the thirteenth century, and Latin in the sixteenth century.[20] He seems to have influenced medieval thought primarily through the Arabic philosophers and possibly also through Proclus. As you may know, Aristotle referred to an active intellect that sparked intellectual activity in more passive intellects, namely humans. We don't really know what he meant by the active intellect, but we do know that for Aristotle the object of God's thought could only be God since nothing else would be worthy of it (Aristotle, *Metaphysics*, XII: 9).

A hybrid Aristotelian/Neoplatonic model became a common theme in medieval philosophy. According to that model, consciousness is actually the origin of the material world. There are many ways of interpreting Aristotle and the early medieval systems tended to misinterpret him (as Themistius might have), because Aristotle believed in an eternal physical universe whereas they believed in a creator God. But despite that rather significant disagreement and Aristotle's incipient concept of consciousness, it is safe to say that neither Aristotle, Themistius, nor their medieval disciples, viewed intelligence as emerging from inert matter. This is what Themistius says: "He intellects all the existents not as being external to His nature and alien to Him. For He is he that generates and creates them, and they are He. . . . The First Intellect intellects the world. For, when intellecting His own Self, He intellects that which He is. From His own Self He intellects that He is the cause and the *Arché* of all things."[21]

The significance of this model, particularly to the Moslem world, should not be underestimated. The Moslem theologians tended to be occasionalists who did not believe in natural necessity or eternal forms. Some even questioned logical necessity. Instead, they viewed all events as arising from the inscrutable will of God. This work was translated into Arabic at the highpoint of early Islamic civilization when intellectual discussion in these areas was further advanced than in the West. The model undercuts occasionalism without denying theism and provides a basis for laws of nature by considering the efficient cause of the physical world (God) to be its formal and final cause as well. According to this model, it is not consciousness but *physicality* that has a hard problem; God, the *Arché*, explains everything else. The model is not necessarily wedded to biblical creationism, though compatible with it, but could be combined with a kind of emanationist view.[22] To see how influential the Arabic translation was, consider this quote from the great eleventh century Moslem philosopher Avicenna. "One of the things that Themistius did well was to show clearly that the first *Arché* intellects His own Self, and then from His own Self He intellects all things. . . . He does not intellect things as being outside of His own Self, intellecting then in themselves as we do with regard to the *sensibilia*, but intellects then in His own Self." (Avicenna, 26–27)

Thomas Aquinas seems to have been influenced by Themistius through Maimonides' *Guide of the Perplexed*. The following quotation is reminiscent of Themistius because, in it, Aquinas stresses God's formal and final causality, and not efficient causality, as proof that God creates all things. "Moreover, as we proved above, God is the maker of things inasmuch as He is in act. But by virtue of His actuality and perfection God embraces all the perfections of things, as was shown in Book I; and thus He is virtually all things. He is, therefore, the maker of all things." (Aquinas, 48)

Gersonides, a fourteenth century Jewish philosopher, was also influenced by Themistius. Gersonides wrote: "He knows only Himself and in this knowledge He knows all things with respect to their general natures. For He is the principle of law, order, and regularity in the universe."[23] He goes on, in good medieval fashion, to assert that this is the true opinion of Aristotle. The fifteenth century Christian philosopher Nicholas of Cusa was also influenced by Themistius, probably through Maimonides' discussion in the *Guide of the Perplexed*, of God being the efficient, formal, and final cause of the universe (Maimonides, 168). Cusanus wrote: "Est igitur Deus causa efficiens et formalis atque finalis omnium, qui efficit in verbo uno omnia quantumcumque diversa inter se."[24] (Therefore God is the efficient and formal and final cause of everything, he who in one word makes everything, however different these things are from each other.)

A closer inspection of Maimonides' argument for the existence of God in *The Guide of the Perplexed* (I, 69) will reveal the power of Themistius' view and how appealing it was to Aristotelians, even though it distorted Aristotle's actual views on the matter. Maimonides begins by saying that God is the efficient, formal, and final cause of all events in the world and of the world itself. He then refers to God as the form of the universe in the Aristotelian sense but cautions that this description should not be taken quite literally. The important thing, he says, is that if you take away the form of something, that entity disappears (and this does seem to be the opinion of Aristotle). He also refers to the relationship between God and the universe as a kind of overflow. Finally he comes to the crux of the matter. Those who argue that you can assume for argument's sake that there is no God and still discuss the universe are completely wrong. They think of God as a maker who can pass away yet his creations remain.

> Now that which they have mentioned would be correct if He were only the maker. . . . Now as He, may he be exalted, is also the form of the world, as we have made clear, and as He continually endows the latter with permanence and constant existence, it would be impossible that He who continually endows with permanence should disappear and that which is continually endowed by Him and which has no permanence except in virtue of this endowment should remain. This is the measure of the vain imagining necessitated by the opinion that He is only a maker and not an end or a form. (Maimonides, 171)

Perhaps we are now able to put all this medieval verbiage into perspective in terms of consciousness studies. Substitute consciousness for God and you get something like a Berkeleyan argument. If there is no God (Creative Consciousness) that which we think of as reality (the physical universe) disappears because it has no inherent permanence.[25] Now I don't mean to imply that this medieval view is the same as subjective idealism. It is not, because it is still very dependent upon Aristotelian and Platonic notions of form despite its inclusion of some subjective elements. But both views challenge the facile and intuitive assumption that I have earlier termed the physicality bias and which lies behind so much of our thinking about reality.

We have seen that all those medieval thinkers considered the physical universe to be causally dependent upon God in a very broad sense that included efficient, formal, and final causality. In fact, they all exceeded Aristotle's original proposal and this can be attributed to Neoplatonic and/or biblical influences. Yet none of them considered the physical world to be God and this also can be ascribed to those same influences. What would happen if you added physicality or material causality to God? You would then have a complete identification of God with the universe, which is what Spinoza actually did.[26]

Now why do I believe that this medieval model is ultimately more explanatory (in a metaphysical sense) than either neutral monism or panpsychism? It seems to me that the being of neutral monism lacks broad causal powers precisely because it is so neutral. Power requires some well developed attributes. Otherwise (if it did have such powers) we might as well say that the ultimate reality is God and monism would become pantheism. The being of panpsychism is also powerless, as its original state must have lacked any of the sophisticated powers that we associate with intelligent beings or even living beings. And if that apparent powerlessness is an illusion, we might as well call it God as well. In other words, both panpsychism and neutral monism tend towards pantheism but neither takes the decisive step that would offer a truly satisfying explanatory scheme. In addition, panpsychism and neutral monism fail to explain why only parts of the universe seem to have consciousness. The transcendental theistic view, on the other hand, finds the origin of consciousness in the transcendent divine mind and then traces it to subordinate mental structures.[27] This explains why some things in the lower world are conscious and some are not and perhaps why some have freedom and others do not.

IS THIS VIEW CONSISTENT WITH MODERN SCIENCE?
It might be argued that all this talk of broad causal powers is antithetical to the modern scientific spirit that only seeks out universal laws and antecedent efficient causes. In other words, science doesn't demand the kind of ultimate understanding that my model (or for that matter panpsychism/neutral monism) proposes to provide. What is wrong with that view? There is really nothing wrong with it. Efficient causes are not good explanations for *why* an event occurs if what we mean by *why* is: Why is the event precisely the way it is? In that sense neuron firings can never really explain why we experience anything specifically, even though they may explain why we have some experiences

and not others. But given the physicality bias, consciousness cries out for explanation or understanding: hence the hard problem. Scientists, however, need not deal with that problem if they don't want to.[28]

CONCLUSION

All of the models that I have described go beyond efficient causality and offer a vision of what reality ultimately is; but there are significant differences in how the models ask one to view that reality. Panpsychism asks us to believe consciousness is ubiquitous and from time immemorial, existing even where it doesn't seem to exist. Neutral monism asks us to believe there is only one reality, completely different from the realities that we think we know about. Both of those models are popular among those who have rejected the notion of a transcendent creator God. Panpsychism might even appear to be a return to a much more primitive type of religiosity but perhaps it can be reconciled with modern science. Neutral monism, since Spinoza, has often been favored by scientifically minded people. The transcendent model that I described does not interfere with our beliefs about physical and mental reality but also asks us to believe in another reality that we can't know much about. Ultimately, acceptance of those models rests on a subjective evaluation of plausibility, but interestingly there is a feature of the transcendent model that may actually indirectly commend itself to scientific thought.

Modern theoretical science developed only in the West, not in ancient Greece or the other great cultures of the ancient world, not in India, China, or the Middle East. Of course, most of those civilizations had their own forms of rationalism and empirical investigation. But none can compare to modern science in effectiveness and ability to adapt and grow. The belief in a transcendent deity and in the existence of two realities (natural and supernatural) may have freed the material world from the enchantment of the religious consciousness and allowed it to be investigated in a dispassionate scientific manner.[29] It would be ironic if such a model, never really favored by intellectuals, should have proven itself so scientifically productive.

We may lament the sometimes acrimonious relationship between religion and science in the West, but we should be at least equally mindful of the fact that in other cultures science never even attained the strength to challenge religion. Of course, I am only speaking from a historical perspective and secularism is at least as logically compatible with science as any religion (and probably more so). It is for that reason that scientists in a free secular society tend not to be religious. But it is truly amazing how many successful scientists do hold religious beliefs, and that would tend to be even more prevalent in more religious societies.

We should be wary of religious litmus tests in either philosophy or science, but we should also be aware of how religious and metaphysical views impact on scientific progress. From a purely logical perspective, a scientist should not be influenced by his or her religious beliefs, yet we know that scientists, like other people, are not purely logical. One of the uses of metaphysics is to suggest scientific theories, and since we only have finite intellectual resources, such suggestions can either advance or retard scientific progress. It is even possible that metaphysical views, such as neutral monism or panpsychism, might retard scientific progress by confusing the extended material world (and its efficient causality) with the ultimate reality and the ultimate explanations for which the human spirit yearns.

Is there a sense, then, in which those theories are true? I think that they could both be incorporated into a more adequate ontology and I will briefly sketch how that is possible. One of the problems that made Themistius' model so popular was the need to reconcile divine omnipotence with the working out of natural laws because an all-powerful God might seem to be a lawless or even whimsical one. Ultimately, some rather complicated relationship must be forged between physicality and divine consciousness if that goal is to be achieved. Otherwise, the apparent lawfulness of the physical world would turn out to be an illusion. In fact, the complexity of such a metaphysic renders it useless as a model for scientific theorizing, which always strives for parsimony. This will also help us see why panpsychism and neutral monism are so popular in a scientific age. They are simple schemes that more closely resemble scientific models.

While most scientists don't feel the need to reconcile laws of nature with an omnipotent God, many desire to reconcile causality with freedom. In order to do that effectively, we may need to stop thinking about one reality and admit the possibility of levels of reality. In the kind of metaphysics that I have in mind there would be one neutral emanation that could not be characterized as either mind or matter. Its bifurcation would be ultimately comprehensible in terms of a yet higher reality. There would be a sense in which mind pervades the physical universe and this would be an inevitable consequence of its ultimate origin in the divine being. I will present such a metaphysical view in the next chapter.

But only when certain phenomenological conditions are met can we really speak of consciousness in the more modern sense of the word. Any model that is taken from a previous age will have to be adapted to these modern requirements. Therefore, the model that I will propose, while having certain advantages, hardly tells us what we really need to know. It merely points towards a phenomenological investigation into what actually constitutes consciousness as well as a more normal scientific investigation into the requirements of a physical structure if it is to possess it. Such exhaustive studies have yet to be done. Perhaps they require a more unified conception of human consciousness, something that I will argue for in Chapter Six.

NOTES

1. See G.R. Evans, 1993, 74: "It is taken as axiomatic that the cause is superior to the effect in the hierarchy of being."
2. Interestingly, Aristotle also recognized that experience, which he derived from imagination and memory, gives a person a kind of knowledge of particulars that causal knowledge does not, and is therefore superior in areas of practical action. Nevertheless, for him true knowledge is not knowledge of particulars but general knowledge of causes. See *The Metaphysics*, I: 1.
3. See Damasio, 2003, 268–70.
4. Chalmers, 1996, xii.
5. Sutherland, 2000, 80.

6. Evolutionary theory allows for many useless forms and organs with such concepts as genetic drift, hitch hiking, neutral evolution, etc. and allows for useful formations that were not adaptations with the concept of spandrels. See Gould and Lewontin, 1978.

7. Consciousness would have to be viewed as so distinct that it couldn't be explained by means of the mechanisms mentioned in the previous footnote.

8. Not all *why* questions are off limits in science. It is perfectly scientific to inquire why certain neuron firings correlate with certain experiences if what is meant by *why* is a search for a theoretical explanation. Once an explanation is provided, if one were still to ask why, it would not be a scientific question. In other words, science does not provide ultimate understanding, but only provisional explanation.

9. Owen Flanagan argues that "it is pretty close to being uncontroversial that sensory consciousness is an adaptation and that awareness of our sensory states is used in guiding action" (Flanagan, 2000, 102). The key words here are *awareness* and *sensory*. Perhaps a creature could have evolved that had sensory awareness and feedback mechanisms without the inner life that we call consciousness. There is evidence from blindsight patients that such unconscious mechanisms might be functionally inferior to conscious ones, but on the other hand, we are often well served by unconscious visual perception. And non-sensory consciousness does not seem nearly as fitness enhancing as sensory awareness. Therefore, I question his conclusion that consciousness is definitely a fitness enhancing adaptation. But even if Flanagan is right, some people still insist on arguing that since zombies are conceivable, therefore they are naturally possible and we need to know why there are no zombies. Now, even if zombies were naturally possible, that does not guarantee their appearance on the stage of evolutionary history. But the question about zombies is not a meaningless one even if it is not crucial to a technical evolutionary explanation of consciousness. Imagine a time when organisms were unconscious, and then all of a sudden one emerges with consciousness which confers upon it a survival advantage. Somehow this even seems to be a much bigger story than the arrival of a creature with a larger brain that can do better unconscious computations. It raises philosophical questions. I think the question of why there is consciousness is an important metaphysical problem similar to the question of why there is something rather than nothing.

10. Damasio, 2003, 206–07.

11. Another interesting point is that if you really believe in neutral monism then you don't need to find efficiencies in consciousness—since it wasn't really produced by evolution.

12. See Gregory, 1989, 27, where the two concepts are equated.

13. See Stubenberg, 1998, 304–06, for a good discussion.

14. See Chalmers, 1996, 299, where he admits this but states that "naturalistic dualism with psychophysical laws" is at the foundation of his view. At the end of the book, he admits that he is only weakly confident regarding panpsychism.

15. Many philosophers and scientists would disagree. For example, El-Hani and Pereira call ontological physicalism "one of the main tenets of the scientific worldview" but give no argument to support it. They also state that ontological physicalism is "one of the main tenets of emergentism." Both of these assertions are justified by "the causal closure of the physical." See Hardcastle, 1999, 333, 339. I have encountered this assertion quite often in philosophical treatises and scientific textbooks, almost always without a supporting argument. Perhaps a convincing argument could once have been made, but given the accumulating data from quantum physics it is becoming increasingly more difficult to do so. The formulas of ontological physicalism and causal closure of the physical seem to me to be empty formalisms that are perfectly compatible with almost any metaphysical view including subjective idealism. The concept of causal closure of the physical encounters additional problems. Historical and biological realities are physical, but we ordinarily think that they cannot be reduced to the laws of physics. Nevertheless, the methodological principle that I alluded to remains intact, and for that reason some of the more exotic interpretations of quantum theory appear to me to be scientifically suspect. I would argue that science does not really have any ontological principles (analogous to religious dogma) such that a denial of them would doom the scientific enterprise or render it unintelligible. But I think this is an area where everyone has to make "a subjective plausibility judgment" (in the words of David Chalmers).

16. Plato expressed disapproval of Homer's mythology because it attributed disgraceful actions to the gods. This raises an important issue that cannot be dealt with adequately here. From one theoretical perspective our beliefs about the gods are projections of our self-consciousness but from another perspective our notion of humanity is dependent upon beliefs about the gods. The problem with mythology is never that it is literally false (it always is) but often centers upon ethical considerations. It is often on that basis that we reject metaphysical beliefs and call them mythological in a pejorative sense.

17. Anthony Freeman, editor of *The Journal of Consciousness Studies*, noted the resemblance of this view to Berkeleyan idealism. However, where Berkeley began with subjective idealism and ended up with God guaranteeing the stability and continuity of the universe, the view that I will describe assumes an objective foundation for subjectivity in the self-consciousness of God as a means of understanding both subjectivity and an ordered universe. It does of course resemble idealism in seeing mind and consciousness

as primary and not derived from physicality, and I will have more to say about this. Views such as idealism emerged out of these medieval traditions.

18. See Chalmers, 1996, 170, where he refers to "spiritualistic, religious, supernatural, and other anti-scientific overtones" of dualism, and uses the term "forces of darkness" to refer to those anti-scientific views.

19. By some definitions, of course, Themistius is not a medieval thinker, but I am primarily concerned with the use of his model by later medieval thinkers.

20. While there is a distinction to be made between knowledge and consciousness, self-knowledge seems to me to be intimately related to consciousness. Themistius considered whether God could be the "Principle and Source of life" yet be like "a man possessed of knowledge who sleeps and does not use his knowledge" and found that alternative absurd. (See Pines, 1996, 272–73). Further evidence that Themistius is referring to experience can be found on p. 273, where he asserts that just as it is preferable for "sight not to be informed of (certain) things," the first intellect would only intellect the "things that are of the utmost excellence." This seems to be a separate argument from the one that asserts that the cause of intellection cannot be inferior to its effect.

21. Pines, 1996, 278. The term *Arché* goes back to pre-Socratic thinkers and originally referred to the stuff out of which the universe is composed. Eventually it came to refer to formal, final, or efficient cause, but not material cause. Themistius employs it here in all three senses and states this explicitly in another part of the commentary. He also refers to God as the *nomos* of the universe, even likening God to a human ruler. This may be metaphorical, however, since for him, even the celestial intelligences that are attached to the heavenly bodies are devoid of sensation or contact with matter, and God must be even more removed. It is a bit of a mystery, therefore, how God could be an efficient cause of events in the physical universe.

22. For a description of Maimonides' esoteric view of emanation and creation, see Gluck, 1998, 226.

23. Gersonides, 1987, 90.

24. Nicholas of Cusa, 1954, II, 9.

25. Obviously, one should not equate God with human consciousness, but it could be argued that this peculiar phenomenon is an emanation from God or a clouded, inferior version of the divine reality.

26. Spinoza accepted the argument of medieval rationalists that God cannot be a body (*corpus*) but rejected their arguments that God cannot be corporeal substance (*substantia corporea*). There is some dispute, therefore, regarding whether Spinoza's system is panpsychic, neutral monist, or neither. See Wolfson, 1977, 593–600. The vast majority of scholars agree that he was a neutral monist, however.

27. While a literal traditionalist view (such as that of Descartes) would confine consciousness to humans, there is no reason why the transcendent view could not be combined with an evolutionary view of the development of consciousness in animals.

28. That assertion may need to be qualified because biologists at times seem to use teleological language. The theory of evolution does not allow us to predict future events nearly as much as it provides us with a plausible explanatory scheme (although some small degree of prediction can be eked out of the theory). Often we speak of the functional modifications of animals through evolution as if it were a conscious design problem rather than simply a process of random trial and error. In fact there are inherent problems with the concept of function. While we can't deal with those problems in any depth here, it might be useful to point out that the equating of scientific explanation with prediction is somewhat narrow and not in accordance with a great deal of the history of science. Nevertheless, the two concepts do seem to be permanently wedded to one another. Therefore, the boundary between science and metaphysics may be somewhat hazy though more extreme cases are easy to categorize. Evolution seems to be a legitimate scientific theory, but the uses that some have put it to can be characterized as metaphysical. For good discussions of some of these issues, see Hardcastle, 1999.

29. It could also be argued that the tendency towards occasionalism in Islamic thought, as exemplified by al-Ghazali, retarded the free growth of science, even though the Islamic world began with many intellectual advantages over the West. Science requires some notion of an inherent lawfulness and stability in the physical universe. While Averroes and some other Islamic thinkers supported such a notion, in general it played a more prominent role in Christian and Jewish thought than it did in Islamic theology.

Chapter Four

Spiritual Matter and Neutral Monism in Solomon ibn Gabirol

Since the intellectual part of man is, of all that he has, the best, that which is most important for him to seek is science. Regarding science, that which is most necessary for him to know is himself, in order that by this knowledge he should also know the things that are outside of himself, because his essence is to understand it and penetrate it all and all those things are subject to his dominion. With this he should also seek the science of the final cause for which he has been created, in order that he should apply himself abundantly to it, for in this way is happiness to be obtained.

—Solomon ibn Gabirol, *Fons Vitae*

We have seen that both scientific and aesthetic viewpoints often favor monism, albeit of different kinds. On the other hand, theological speculation seems to favor idealism and, as will be shown in the next chapter, the ordinary epistemic intuition of modernity and of the social sciences favors dualism. I will now present a medieval model in which neutral monism is combined with theism, idealism, and dualism. It has certain advantages in terms of reconciling conflicting intuitions about reality, but the reader must be warned in advance that it may be difficult to understand and perhaps even more difficult to accept. Nevertheless, it is generally acknowledged to be one of the great creative accomplishments of medieval philosophy.

Solomon ibn Gabirol was a Spanish Jew who lived in the eleventh century. For most of the history that has elapsed since his rather brief life, he has been misunderstood. In fact, his literary productions that survived were bifurcated under the names of two completely separate authors: Avicebron and Shelomo ibn Gabirol. The former was a mysterious philosopher whose metaphysical work, the *Fons Vitae*, was read by the Scholastics in a Latin translation from the original Arabic. The latter was one of the greatest poets of the synagogue. His magnificent Hebrew poems are read by Sephardic Jews on the High Holy Days as well as on many other occasions. It was not until the nineteenth century that Salomon Munk found a fragment of the *Fons Vitae*, in the Library of Paris, that had been translated into Hebrew by a later philosopher and attributed to ibn Gabirol. From that time on, we have known the true identity of that mysterious Avicebron. His beliefs had caused quite a stir in Medieval Christian Europe and Thomas Aquinas called the *Fons Vitae* (Fountain of Life) a poisoned well, perhaps alluding to its flirtation with monism and pantheism. But few of the Jews who read his poetry ever imagined that there was anything very controversial about his thoughts. In hindsight, however, we can now see many deep philosophical concepts in his poetry. And there was at least one prominent Jewish family, the Abrabanels, who seem to have known who Avicebron really was.[1] But that is another story and I will focus here on what is perhaps the strangest and most innovative concept in the *Fons Vitae*: spiritual matter, which appears to me to be neutral monist in nature. I will also attempt to show how his metaphysics incorporates neutral monism on the highest levels (beyond corporeality), idealism on the intermediary level, and dualism (mind and matter) on the lower levels.[2]

We tend to think of matter as a heavy inert substance that seems far removed from spirituality, as the popular term *materialistic* implies. As I have argued earlier, even when we adopt neutral monism as a conceptual scheme, it is difficult for us to really get away from that gross corporeal stuff. For ibn Gabirol, however, that stuff to which I just alluded would be better described as corporeality and it is only one kind of matter: the lowest kind. For example, he believed that angels were also composed of a higher kind of matter. If we utilize the Aristotelian notion of matter and form, as he did, we can approximate the views of ibn Gabirol but we should keep in mind that, for Aristotle, matter was a great deal less substantial than it was for him. Let us imagine matter with no form at all—prime matter. For Aristotle this would be mere potentiality. He had inherited from his teacher Plato a kind of contempt for matter. He was also a rather down to earth thinker and perhaps could hardly imagine a completely non-corporeal matter. Even his heavenly ether has extension and therefore could be considered physical. So for Aristotle, matter, while not complete nothingness, lacked substantiality in the absence of form and can best be described as potentiality. But for ibn Gabirol, spiritual matter is the most real thing of all (aside from God) and is a direct, albeit complex, emanation from the divinity. How can this be?

One of the most interesting and controversial features of ibn Gabirol's theology is his division of God into two distinct aspects. Of course, in an ultimate metaphysical sense God is one, but these two aspects represent distinct ways in which we can approach the ultimate divine reality. Perhaps this explains why Christians took a far greater interest in this part of his thought than did Jews. The two aspects can be described as Divine Will and (for lack of a better term) Divine Essence. When we speak of the Divine Will in this context we don't just mean God's plan for human behavior or contingent worldly events. We mean any and all interventions or causal relationships between God and any other reality. Therefore, everything in this world (or any other world) is the product of the Divine Will. This is a basic metaphysical category and we can't have any other reality without it.

What Aristotle called *Form* is (for ibn Gabirol) the immediate product of that Divine Will. Does that mean that both the world and spiritual reality as we know them are simply the whimsical creations of a powerful will? We will not explore deeply the perplexing relationship between intellect and will but the short answer according to ibn Gabirol is no. Will is indeed higher than intellect in his system but it is not without direction. For ibn Gabirol the Divine Will functions to a great extent in accordance with something even higher—the Divine Essence (which could also be termed the Divine Wisdom). That notion resolves one of the greatest problems facing Arabic philosophy: reconciling divine freedom and omnipotence with the apparently lawful governance of the universe. This bifurcation of God into Will and Essence also resolves the duality regarding Mind and Will by regarding God as a neutral substance (so to speak) regarding that duality. It also points to the relationship between God and other realities, following from the very nature of the deity. This is the most controversial part of his thought because it tends towards pantheism and it is the opinion of many that Spinoza obtained many of his ideas from this source.

We have noted the Divine Will as giving form or direction to every reality outside of God but we might still want to know what gives those things reality. For Platonists, they are not quite real at all but only participate in the Forms (which are sometimes interpreted as ideas in the divine mind). The traditional religious answer is that God calls things into existence out of sheer nothingness or thinks them into existence. The Aristotelian answer might be that form or essence gives substance or reality to composite material entities, which is a more common-sense modification of the Platonic view. But for Neoplatonists like ibn Gabirol, those are not very good answers.

From nothingness, nothing of substance comes, which leads to the unacceptable conclusion that this earthly reality is really a kind of illusion. That was the conclusion to a certain extent of Hindu philosophers and Plato, but it is unacceptable from a biblical perspective, just as it was unacceptable to Aristotle. For ibn Gabirol, however, there must be some quasi-divine substance that lends reality to the whole process of creation because the biblical view precludes the Aristotelian solution—an eternal physical universe. That metaphysically needed substance is spiritual matter and it comes from God. Form also comes from God—from the Divine Will—but spiritual matter is even higher as it is related to the Divine Essence itself. And like God (so to speak) it is a neutral substance: neutral regarding the next three levels of matter: intellect, soul, and corporeality, the latter two being the familiar Cartesian duality.[3] Now many readers are probably thinking that all this sounds a little or a lot like the kind of pantheism associated with Spinoza, but there is a crucial difference.

We have seen that the Divine Will gives direction to the world through an intermediary—form. Likewise, the Divine Essence gives reality to the world through an intermediary—matter. Therefore, matter is not the Divine Essence any more than form is. In fact, at times he describes matter as a creation of the Divine Will, but here there seems to be an incongruity. Strictly speaking, creation occurs only after universal form unites with universal matter. Anything prior to that might better be described metaphysically as emanation. But this is a rather complex kind of emanation from the Divine Essence. We said previously that all relationships between God and any other reality are governed by the Divine Will. Therefore, we can't say that universal matter is simply a simple emanation from the Divine Essence. Something changes radically when you go from the Divine Essence to universal matter. We can conceptualize universal matter as substance and foundation of the created universe, but the Divine Essence is really beyond conceptualization at all. Nevertheless, matter is a very high and spiritual reality and closer to the divine reality than is form. That is because form is an extension of the Divine Will, which is likened to a divine artisan while matter is an extension of the Divine Essence itself. Hence, what ibn Gabirol has done is to turn Aristotle on his head and yet there remains a certain resemblance.

For Aristotle, matter was mere potentiality. In his poetry ibn Gabirol describes matter as the shadow of the divine reality. Isaac Israeli (another early Jewish philosopher) and Plotinus also used the metaphor of light and shade to describe emanation. For Plotinus, *shadow* was the equivalent of image or imitation. Shadow is not a particularly favorable term. Compared with the divine reality, however, nothing can be favorably described. Yet that shadow is generally the highest reality that we could ever know (at least in this life). If we could actually apprehend the divine reality itself, we might cease to exist—a result the Moslem mystics sometimes alluded to. Therefore, those who superficially read ibn Gabirol as a monist or pantheist, and consequently compare him to the pluralists of the Christian West, are perhaps mistaken. His intellectual background is both monist and pluralist. The rabbis and Aristotle were pluralists while the Moslem mystics were often monists. He seems dissatisfied with both and his metaphysics is an attempt to overcome the limitations of each, bridging the gap between creation and emanation.

Now that we have made clear that universal matter is not God, we can attempt to understand how elevated a spiritual substance it really is. He also calls it the Throne of Glory, a very ancient term from Jewish mysticism. It is the foundation and it is a mystery. It is so high that only the saints who have died can approach it and even they are nested under it. The angels apparently cannot approach it. Despite that, it is also the substratum from which everything ultimately emerges. Hence, it is both transcendent and immanent. It is the stuff out of which the creation is made yet only intellectual substance emerges directly from it. The human soul, like the angels, is composed of that intellectual substance and I will now discuss that very briefly.

The Divine Will creates something called universal form. But perhaps *creates* is the wrong word as this may really be a kind of emanation. Universal Matter emanates from the Divine Essence (even though the Divine Will is said to be involved). Universal Form, however, is purely an extension of the Divine Will. When Universal Form unites with Universal Matter, something called Intellect emerges. This is also called the Sphere of Intellect. That intellectual realm is the origin of everything else. It is the mental stuff out of which the human soul and the angels are directly created. It is also the stuff out of which everything else is created, albeit indirectly via the form of corporeality. So we can see that this philosopher was not afflicted by the physicality bias.

He also did not view the human mind as an orphan in a corporeal universe—sustained only by the weakest relationship to God but estranged from the rest of God's creation. Instead, the entire universe, physical and mental, is under the direct rule of this Intellectual sphere.

So to summarize I will give a list of substances going from the lowest to the highest. I may have skipped a substance between corporeality and intellectuality but it is not crucial to our discussion. The list is as follows. After each substance I indicate whether it is neutral monistic, dualistic or idealistic.

Corporeal substance	Dualistic (entities composed of minds and physical matter)
Soul substance	Dualistic (entities composed of minds and non-physical matter)
Intellectual substance	Idealistic (pure intellectual substance with forms but no entities)
Universal matter	Monistic (substance beyond intellect)
Divine Essence	Monistic (beyond substance)

Each substance emerges out of the next highest substance with the aid of a different form. As you can see, matter here is a true substance as is the soul. The great duality on the lowest level is soul/corporeality. Intellectual substance, from which emerge both soul and body, is a splendid example of idealism. Universal Matter is perhaps the best example that we have in medieval philosophy of neutral monism. In short, whereas Aristotle gives priority to form over matter, ibn Gabirol reverses that ranking. You can see from this that for him matter was very spiritual indeed. The divine essence is perhaps another example of monism but one must beware of the pitfalls in considering it to be substance.[4] The divine will/essence is not a duality; the former emerges out of the latter.

This leads to another interesting aspect of his thought. Despite its intellectualist leanings and its reliance upon spiritual matter for the substantial reality of the universe, will is accorded a very high role in the system: even higher than intellect. This raises an important issue. If indeed ibn Gabirol reverses the Aristotelian bias towards form in favor of matter, what is the role of form in his system? It does not lend substantial reality to things as it does in Plato and Aristotle. Yet it does guarantee the individuality of things, particularly of human beings. So in the final analysis, individuality is saved from monism by the operation of the Divine Will in accordance with the unknowable Divine Wisdom.

Regarding his influence upon more modern thinkers, it would be almost entirely indirect. This was always his fate, with the exception of the Christian Scholastics and certain Kabbalists. It has been suggested that he may have influenced Giordano Bruno and Spinoza. The concept of intelligible or spiritual matter certainly resembles neutral monism and panpsychism: modern answers to the consciousness problem. That problem, I repeat, regards how it is possible for consciousness to exist in a material universe. The problem, of course, presupposes a debunking of the Cartesian solution, which even Descartes himself probably felt uncomfortable with. Neutral monism argues that ultimate reality is neither physical nor mental and this coheres with ibn Gabirol's spiritual matter, which is ontologically prior to intellect and even more so to corporeality. Panpsychism argues that consciousness must go all the way down to the earliest appearance of matter if it is not to be explained away in a reductionist fashion. The spiritual matter of ibn Gabirol would seem to have the capacity for consciousness but his corporeal matter might not. Therefore, one cannot view his system as panpsychist. Nevertheless, corporeal matter in his system emerges from soul substance and might retain some traces of consciousness.

CONCLUSION

Solomon ibn Gabirol, one of the most inventive medieval metaphysicians, wanted to reconcile the apparent dualities of the phenomenal world and Aristotelian hylomorphism with the monistic conceptions of the Neoplatonists and mystics of the Arab world. His metaphysics attempts to resolve the respective problems of dualism, idealism, and neutral monism by combining them all in a series of levels of reality. On the one hand, it preserves some element of divine voluntarism with its prominent conception of the Divine Will. On the other hand, it includes all of reality in the neutral monistic spiritual matter that emanates from God. The danger of all monistic schemes is the loss of the individual. He resolves that problem by positing a Divine Essence and Wisdom that is even beyond the monistic reality of matter. Ultimately, then, the mystery of individuality and freedom is justified by a more or less traditional religious faith.

NOTES

1. Judah Abrabanel alludes to it in his *Dialoghi d'Amore*, which leads one to suspect that it might have been common knowledge among Jewish intellectuals, kabbalists, etc. in the Renaissance—or, perhaps, only within the Abrabanel family.

2. Additional information regarding ibn Gabirol can be obtained in any good history of Jewish philosophy, the *Jewish Encyclopedia*, *Encyclopedia Judaica*, etc. The best example of his philosophical poetry is the Kingly (Royal) Crown. See the Bernard Lewis translation, recently expanded with additional philosophical commentary.

3. I have referred to God a number of times as a neutral substance, for the sake of simplicity, but that is not quite correct since many mystics and philosophers, such as Plotinus, consider God to be beyond Being altogether. I cannot say for sure whether that was the opinion of ibn Gabirol. He sometimes speaks of God as being beyond Being and sometimes as Being itself. On the one hand, a God equated with Being lends itself to mysticism while a God beyond Being does not. But on the other hand, many mystics speak of union with God as an experience of nothingness. There is some debate regarding the mystical nature of ibn Gabirol's thought. Perhaps it only goes so far as spiritual matter while the God beyond Being remains for him the unknowable yet yearned-for God of faith.

4. That is because the category of substance pertains to the created universe and not really to God.

Chapter Five

Descartes and Spinoza

That which follows is not by any means an exhaustive account of the lives or beliefs of either of these thinkers—Descartes and Spinoza. There is no lack of literature for that. Instead, I have chosen to give short accounts of their religious lives and to suggest how their religious beliefs might have interacted with their scientific and metaphysical views. Along with other texts, I have utilized, and would highly recommend, *The Career of Philosophy* by John Herman Randall, Jr. He was a master at relating medieval, Renaissance, and modern philosophies to one another. I disagree with him, however, on the extent to which modern scientific models refute Cartesian dualism.

Renè Descartes and Baruch Spinoza were both heirs to the great medieval syntheses as well as being forgers of modern thought. Both attempted to reconcile religion and science, but in somewhat different fashions. Descartes allowed himself to look at the world at times as if God did not exist even though he sincerely believed that He did exist. In the end, however, that method made him even more reliant upon the traditional God of religion, even if he had somewhat idiosyncratic views about Him. Spinoza, on the other hand, refused to separate science from religion, which made him an outcast from his religious community and also incapable of joining another. In the end, he abandoned the traditional God of Western religion and came to worship the absolute substance of neutral monism.

DESCARTES

When I first began to study philosophy, I was taught that Descartes was the first modern philosopher. Prior to him were the medieval philosophers who worked in the service of religion and did not employ critical rational thought. After spending many years studying medieval philosophy and Descartes, I can no longer agree with that assessment. I am not even sure why Descartes should be called a modern philosopher in contrast to the medieval and Renaissance thinkers who preceded him. Perhaps it has to do with the rise of modern science, with which Descartes was so involved. But Descartes was also very concerned with religion despite the fact that he came under heavy attack by religious authorities. Perhaps that is another reason why some call him the first modern philosopher, but we should not forget that Moses Maimonides and Thomas Aquinas were also attacked by religious authorities. At any rate, unless he was a very good deceiver, Descartes was a sincerely religious man. Queen Christina of Sweden attributed her conversion to Roman Catholicism to him.

Descartes was born in France in 1596 and had a good Scholastic education under the Jesuits. He was essentially an Augustinian Neoplatonist and supplemented that tradition with the new mathematical physics. Aside from God and the laws of nature (attributable to the immutable will of God) his other concern (as a good Augustinian) was with the individual human soul. On November 10, 1619, at age 23, his life changed abruptly. He had a dream that he interpreted as a mystic vision. The Angel of Truth told him to trust his intuition that the world is mathematical. This gave religious sanction to his scientific and philosophical work. In gratitude he went on a pilgrimage to Loretto and afterwards devoted his life to that mathematical method. From 1628 to 1649 he lived in Holland, which, as we shall see, was a haven for unusual or unpopular ideas.

It may be easier to understand Cartesian dualism if we keep medieval rationalism and Augustinianism in mind. Although he rejected so much of the Aristotelian philosophy, Descartes continued in the Aristotelian tradition of medieval philosophy in attempting to understand the world in terms of a rational God who is in constant touch with and is never very far removed from the world, but whose immutable will translates into unchanging laws of nature governed by mathematical principles. In a sense, Descartes mathematized the Aristotelian forms. But even the mathematical principles themselves are the result of God's inscrutable will. In that sense (and like many medieval thinkers) he was not a true Aristotelian. In the medieval period, skepticism and fideism were each offered as alternatives to mainstream Aristotelianism. Once Platonic or Aristotelian metaphysics are rejected, a new method of escaping doubt is needed. The only thing that saves Descartes from complete skepticism is his belief in God, albeit one couched in rational "proofs."

The Neoplatonic tradition also retained its hold on Descartes. He began as an Augustinian and never really abandoned that tradition's emphasis on introspection. Far removed from this world of extension, physicality, and motion, there is a divine world of mind that has left a small trace in this world—in the human soul. Descartes definitively reduced the soul to mind by rejecting the animal and vegetable souls in favor of more modern scientific principles of growth and motion. There is still, however, some ambiguity regarding the meaning of *mind*. If we observe a computer or robot in action we might be tempted to say that they have minds. Nevertheless, we might still reject the notion that they have selves. Some resolve this ambiguity by distinguishing between mind and consciousness. One could, for example, imagine a person who, as a result of a psychotropic drug, can no longer think but remains conscious; we also speak about unconscious mental processes as in a computer. Ordinarily we do not need to make this distinction because we are primarily concerned with both conscious and rational mental processes. But it appears to me that the kind of mental process that includes within itself the notion of a self (*Cogito ergo sum*) is always a conscious mental event.

We can know the conscious human mind through our own introspection, as St. Augustine came to know his soul, while the external physical world can only be known through the laws of physics and motion, all governed by mathematics. But in the final analysis, do we really know anything about nature and matter? For Descartes, all of the elegance of mathematical theory in the end tells us nothing about the real nature of matter and causality. It may be the best that the human mind can devise. It may even point to the Author of this world, but ultimately we must resign ourselves to a lack of understanding of why when one billiard ball hits another with a certain force and in a certain direction the result is always the same. Ultimately there is only one completely adequate explanation—the immutable thoughts of God. Hence, beyond the Cartesian ontology of mind and matter lies the unknowable Neoplatonic God. And that is extremely significant.

Whenever Descartes attempts to account for the world of nature as if there was no God it is just that—an "as if" account. The fact that there *is* a God renders all of our knowledge, no matter how glorious, somewhat suspect. And so, in the final analysis, Descartes trusted reason less than some of the more rationalistic medieval philosophers, who could never imagine a conflict between the reasonable and the true or the good. But in a dualistic world of mind and matter such conflict is quite possible, even if God tells one in a dream to forge on with reason.

Descartes is very much a voluntarist. Assent can be denied to almost any proposition, no matter how indubitably true it is. It is only faith in God's benevolence that consistently induces human beings to seek the truth. But since his very belief in God is based upon rational proofs and clear and distinct ideas, that epistemology incurs the charge of circularity. Everything in his system (with the exception of errors endemic to the science of his day) follows from correct premises—everything but his first premise: the existence of God. This perhaps tells us something about the tradition of which Descartes was a vital part.

In 1649 Descartes accepted the invitation of the Queen of Sweden to join her circle of scholars in Stockholm. In 1650 he died of pneumonia. This has been attributed both to the harsh climate and the harsh demands of his patron to get up early in the morning to teach her science and philosophy.

SPINOZA

Baruch Spinoza was born into the Sephardic[1] Jewish community of Amsterdam. Unlike almost all other Jewish communities this was not a traditional one, following beliefs and practices that seem to traditional folk as if they had always been and always will be. This was a marrano[2] community, the product of Spanish and Portuguese Jews who, for one reason or another, had converted to Christianity in the Iberian Peninsula. Some had converted in Spain as early as 1391, others in 1492 and still others in 1498 in Portugal. Many were extremely wealthy, had married into Iberian aristocracy and had served the monarchs of Spain and Portugal. At any rate, by the time they began arriving in the Netherlands in the sixteenth century they hardly knew what Judaism was. And just as their real reasons for converting to Christianity were varied and often unknown, so were their reasons for returning to Judaism in Holland under the relatively tolerant but watchful eye of the Dutch Reformed Church. We do know, however, that this church was much more favorably inclined towards Jews than it was towards Roman Catholics and this may offer a partial explanation. And so these marranos embarked upon the not so easy task of remaking themselves into a Jewish community.[3] They did so under the guidance of rabbis brought in from Morocco, Turkey, and Europe.

As would be expected, these haughty rebellious hidalgos chafed under the strictures of traditional Jewish law and lore. Heresy was rampant. The most celebrated heretical figure prior to Spinoza was Uriel da Costa. Born a Catholic of Jewish ancestry, he became a priest in Portugal but seems to have been sincerely challenged by the dogmas of the church. Deciding to convert to his ancestral Jewish religion, he migrated to Amsterdam but soon found that his new religion seemed contrary to his reason just as the old one had. The story of Uriel da Costa is a tragic one of vain attempts to recant in order to maintain his social status. Everyone in the Amsterdam Jewish community must have known about this tragic episode (ending in suicide), including the then eight-year-old genius, Baruch Spinoza.

Soon enough, Spinoza, the most brilliant student in the Jewish school of Amsterdam, also got into trouble with the rabbis. After leaving the Jewish school he embarked upon the study of contemporary philosophy and science. When he was twenty-four years old, his heretical views became known; he was expelled and excommunicated from the Jewish community. Luckily for him (and unlike Uriel da Costa), he seems to have had little need for a traditional community. In fact, he seems to have been the first person of note to live completely outside of any religious community. A keen student of medieval Jewish philosophy, he believed that the rationalism of that tradition combined with the up to date science of his own time rendered many traditional views unsustainable.

His quasi-heretical views are legion, but for our purposes we will concentrate on his one absolute substance, which he variously termed *God* or *Nature*. This is not the Aristotelian God, functioning as the form of the eternal universe. It is not the Neoplatonic God, far removed from this world and essentially unknowable but leaving clear traces for the discerning. Some, like Randall, argue that Spinoza's God was no farther removed from the God of the Bible than the Aristotelian or Neoplatonic ones. That may well be the case, but certainly it was far less well received by the religious communities (both Jewish and Christian).

Spinoza's God is the very ground of being of the world, the laws of nature, and the human mind. In terms of the medieval views that have been surveyed earlier in this study, it most closely approximates the spiritual matter of ibn Gabirol, but for Spinoza the absolute substance includes corporeality and mind. His arguments for the one eternal substance are reminiscent of ibn Gabirol's arguments for the one prime matter as an emanation from God. Like that spiritualized matter it is immanent and transcendent, potentially mental and physical. It is replete with glory and holiness and therefore no physical evolutionary history can account for its spiritual dimension, which simply *is*.

But for Spinoza (unlike ibn Gabirol) there is no greater One above it. This spiritual matter *is* God. And so Spinoza, from an orthodox Jewish or Christian point of view, ends up committing one of the worst sins of all. He worships not a divine person but a divine thing, albeit the most glorious thing imaginable. Hence some have called him an atheist and others have considered him "God intoxicated."

What follows from Spinoza's rejection of the personal God of the Bible is that the informed judgment of the human mind becomes the absolutely final authority. Although he certainly gives human emotions their due, for Spinoza there is no transcendent God (beyond reason) sitting in judgment over the human scientific enterprise. Therefore, Pascal's solution regarding a God appearing to the human heart was unavailable to him. Less of a scientist than Descartes and Pascal, he was far more impressed with the scientific enterprise. As the name of his book, *The Ethics*, suggests, there is no valid distinction between facts and values, nor can there be, just as there is no distinction between mind and matter or between Nature and God. That which is must also be what is necessary under the inexorable laws of God's Being and, therefore, is also the good.

It would be a mistake to consider Spinoza a physicalist or one who extols emotion at the expense of reason. For him the ultimate reality can be viewed as either mind or matter, and emotions are simply confused ideas. Many of those contemporary thinkers who view him as a precursor of materialism would be shocked by his asceticism, indicating contempt for physicality, and his resemblance to the medieval philosophical tradition. There is a sense in which his pantheism is the logical extension of philosophical trends implicit in Jewish medieval philosophy and Kabbalah. He lived a quiet life, grinding lenses for a living, ostracized by his community of birth but in touch with some of the great minds of his day. He died at age forty-four, possibly of consumption or possibly of lung disease caused by his occupation.

CONCLUSION

Both Descartes and Spinoza were schooled in medieval thought and were highly indebted to the free-wheeling discussions regarding the relationship between God and the world—causality, free will, miracles, etc.—that raged in the medieval schools. Both were religious men, but Spinoza's religiosity seems to have gone over the line in terms of acceptability to revealed religion. Both attempted to integrate the medieval ways of thinking with the new science of their day. Neither would be comfortable with the physicalist orientation of modern thought (despite the fact that Spinoza has been adopted as a hero by some physicalists, possibly because of his explicit challenge to religious orthodoxy).

NOTES

1. The word *Sephardic* sometimes refers to Jews from the Iberian Peninsula and their descendants, but is most often used to refer to almost all Jews from Arab and Moslem countries, of which Iberian Jews originally formed a part. It is sometimes but not always used to refer to native Italian or Greek Jews, but that was certainly not the case in Spinoza's time. It is never used to refer to Ethiopian Jews, but is sometimes used to refer to Persian and Yemenite Jews. It is derived from a biblical place name that some interpreted as referring to Spain but more likely referred to Turkey. I have never seen it used to refer to "those who come from the cities of the south" as Damasio (2003, 234) claims.

2. A Spanish epithet for those Jews who converted. It came to refer to those who practiced crypto-Judaism.

3. I use the term *marrano* advisedly but it has historically been used to describe the Amsterdam Sephardic Jewish community. This traditional view assumes that the inquisition never threatened good Catholics but only crypto-Jews, forcing them to emigrate and re-convert to Judaism. Recent revisionist scholarship questions the traditional assumption that all of the families comprising that community practiced crypto-Judaism in Spain or Portugal, rather than changing religions opportunistically. Damasio (2003, 247–49) accepts the traditional view as a given.

Chapter Six

Consciousness and the Social Sciences

This joke most powerfully states the absurdity of behaviorism as a way of understanding the human reality. Two behaviorists have just made love and one says to the other: That was great for you but how was it for me? Behaviorism is no longer considered the paradigm of what a behavioral science ought to be. It was attacked for its failure to allow for the kind of theoretical fictions that have been found so useful in science, as well as for its reductionist bias that seems to deny human agency as well as consciousness. It gave way to physicalism (in the narrow sense) that attempted to identify consciousness with neural structures and activities in the brain. (This physicalism should not be confused with the broader metaphysical view that all reality is physical—physical monism) That narrow physicalist view was also attacked from a number of perspectives both scientific and philosophical. For example, while certain mental functions are associated with neural activity in particular parts of the brain, after injury to those areas other regions of the brain can sometimes take over the same function.

If I understand Damasio correctly, he is in the physicalist camp, but has gone off the reservation somewhat. He espouses what he calls an *organismic perspective,*[1] which from the point of view of natural science is perhaps the best perspective that there is.

So from a purely scientific point of view, we are in perfect agreement. There is, however, the same *philosophical* objection to physicalism (the equating of consciousness with neurophysiology) that there had been to behaviorism: mental concepts just don't seem to equate to physical ones. Damasio, however, is particularly annoyed at Cartesian dualism and may not share that intuition.[2]

On the other hand, he may be trying to get around this when he states: "feelings are largely constituted by the perception of a certain body state."[3] Descartes also considered emotions (passions) to be perceptions of bodily states.[4] But there are two major problems here. Firstly, the term "perception of a certain bodily state" fails as a non-mental definition of *feeling* since both perception and feeling are mentalistic concepts. So he has certainly not succeeded in showing that a mental concept equates to a physical concept even if this is a good scientific methodological principle.

We are thrown back to the phenomenal contents of feelings that need not be "constituted by" anything to do with my bodily state, though they undoubtedly are (at least partly) *caused* by my bodily state. This misconception may hearken back to the traditional (but no longer cogent) view discussed in chapter three: to know the cause of a phenomenon is to know its essence. The philosophy of science has succeeded in ridding us of such simplistic views of causality without, I must add, giving us anything very viable in its stead. Nevertheless, we must go forward with the results of critical reason even if it is not always pleasant (in philosophy, at any rate).

Functionalism and epiphenomenalism attempt to answer those objections. Epiphenomenalism asserts the ontological reality of consciousness but only as an adjunct to physical reality. It very clearly illustrates what I have earlier termed the physicality bias. Either consciousness always existed as a *property* of matter (panpsychism), or it is an emergent property. In either case it has no real causal efficacy because the physical world is considered to constitute a closed causal system.

Functionalism is far more sophisticated; according to that view, consciousness refers to higher level processing of data and the actual mechanism by which it happens is not crucial to its definition at all.[5] One way of conceptualizing this is with a computer, (many functionalists obtain inspiration from artificial intelligence work). Computers process information. We also receive information through the senses and then act upon it, but prior to acting in a deliberative manner, something else happens; that higher level accessing and processing of data is consciousness, according to functionalism. According to that paradigm, a computer might also be conscious. It is not the computer hardware or electrical activity that constitutes consciousness, however, but the information processing.

Functionalism is certainly a promising paradigm, particularly in psychology.[6] It has the distinct virtue of focusing on what consciousness *does* rather than on what causes it, but it loses sight of what it *feels* like. Some view this blindness as a problem. Many people, moreover, have distaste for the notion that a machine can be conscious. It is even stronger than the reluctance to admit that animals or other forms of life could be conscious. Just why we don't believe machinery to be conscious is not entirely clear but, rightly or wrongly, many people associate consciousness with living things. This association is not simply a popular prejudice but has been asserted by important scholars such as John Searle and Tyler Burge.[7]

At least seven meanings of the term *consciousness* have been identified by Thomas Natsoulas.[8] This proliferation of views has created a problem. At least naive behaviorists *thought* they knew what consciousness was and agreed on how to detect it in others. As Güven Guzeldere has pointed out, those more sophisticated views have resulted in a complete lack of consensus regarding what consciousness is and how it can be detected![9]

Scientists look for fruitful methodological models, and the physicalist and functionalist models are indeed fruitful. But despite that, and despite the obvious interest in differentiating more and more sophisticated views, most appear to me to be a variety of naturalism, which is the attempt to apply the methods of the natural sciences to the study of human beings. I will argue that such models can never really exhaust the human reality.[10]

Hence my first focus in this chapter is to point out the inadequacy of all conceptualizations of consciousness that base themselves on naturalism, reviewing what was done in Chapter One.[11]

While there has been a great deal of talk in consciousness studies about expanding the frontiers of science, those discussions often overlook the fact that there is not just one kind of science. Ever since Kuhn's work became widely known, we have become accustomed to think in terms of research programs in science that are incommensurable, one with another, but there is still something about that notion that is difficult to accept. It has often been argued that Kuhn's view is not correct, at least in the physical sciences. Sam Rakover, for example, thinks that there is no complete discontinuity of theoretical perspectives in the natural sciences but that such "true revolutions" do indeed occur in psychology.[12]

This question may begin to resolve itself once we determine what *kinds* of science are appropriate to the study of consciousness. While the study of physical processes is important, the study of consciousness only really makes sense to me as part of the study of humanity, and we are likely to obtain absurd results if we attempt to separate consciousness from the overall human reality.[13] That reality has sometimes been explored by philosophers, psychologists, and sociologists in a manner involving *Verstehen* (inter-subjective understanding). But in my review of the consciousness literature, I have not found very many attempts to link study of consciousness with the *verstehende* method of the social sciences.[14]

Perhaps we need to put the problem in some historical perspective in order for the human reality to be better understood. Some have argued that the concept of consciousness is of recent vintage. The origin of the consciousness problem is often viewed as a peculiar error of Descartes that has been foisted upon western thought. This is by no means the invention of Antonio Damasio, who follows a host of other thinkers.[15] As proof of the arbitrary nature of the mind-body distinction, it is often argued that the ancient Greeks did not know of a mind-body problem.[16] We have already seen that this was indeed the case to a great extent. But problems related to what we now call consciousness are not particularly modern. Plato, Aristotle, and the Neoplatonists all had theories about the human soul, even if they did not make the radical differentiations that Descartes did.[17] There is, therefore, some difficulty projecting our notion of phenomenal consciousness onto ancient Greek thought, but when we arrive at the medieval period we are on somewhat safer and perhaps much more familiar ground.[18]

In the Middle Ages, religious philosophers tried to reconcile the Aristotelian concept of soul as the form and perfection of the living body with the Neoplatonic notion of soul as a foreign entity from a spiritual realm. This seems suspiciously similar to the debates that we are having today regarding phenomenal consciousness versus functional consciousness. We have indeed seen that Descartes, the champion of phenomenal consciousness, was to some extent an Augustinian Neoplatonist. Those who favor functional aspects of consciousness are perhaps more in tune with the Aristotelian tradition.

Another aspect of medieval philosophy that we reviewed was the extensive and influential discussion of the internal senses by Avicenna and other Arabic philosophers. Some medieval thinkers argued that the soul was a microcosm. Some viewed it as intermediary between the physical and spiritual worlds. Many insisted there were really a number of human souls, some more spiritual than others. Still others insisted on the soul as a unitary entity.

Also related to the mind-body problem, it is indeed the case that many medieval and early modern thinkers (including Descartes) were unimpressed by the causal efficacy of matter due to theological predilections, and this may have led to the Humean view of causality. It should be kept in mind that such theological views about power residing in God could be read as anthropomorphic, as could the alternative realist notion of powerful particulars.[19] In fact, the very concept of power is basically a sociological one.

Medieval philosophy was part of the science of its day. In a similar fashion, modern philosophy is geared to our science even if we now draw a much stronger line between empirical and analytical questions. As there were then, there are a number of ontologies that would work given the present state of empirical knowledge. Though in my view ontologies can't generally be inferred from scientific findings, they surely should not be inconsistent with them. They are interesting and potentially useful models that we can agree upon if we share similar intuitions.[20] But oftentimes natural scientists are little bothered by philosophical discussions. Since they share similar (and often unconscious) intuitions, they either share similar ontological views or don't concern themselves with such matters.

Another solution is to ignore external reality and focus only on human cognition in light of human interests as in the cognitive interest theory of Jürgen Habermas. It surely has validity on the historical/sociological level, though it undermines empirical knowledge by reducing it to the product of a practical, material interest. But if all theories serve some interest, which one does Habermas' theory serve?

Many theoretical sciences did indeed have their initial impetus in serving specific human interests but they later tended to develop autonomously. Many suspect, however, that the universal character of natural science results from the fact that it really does tell us something about the nature of physical reality. This is sometimes called realism—as distinguished from actualism, which only concerns itself with actual external events rather than underlying structures.[21]

I suspect, however, that important aspects of reality are left out of natural science because some of the interests that gave rise to it also limit it. This may partly explain what is known in consciousness studies as the *explanatory gap*.[22] For example, natural science developed as part of the human project of taming nature and it should not surprise us if it knows little of the untamable powers of human creativity.[23] Perhaps the model expounded in chapter three might tell us more about it than natural science can.

THE PROBLEM OF DEFINITION AND DEMARCATION
Before we explore the relationship between consciousness and *Verstehen* it might be important to demarcate the scientific

study of consciousness (in a general way) from other studies of consciousness. This is important because most people would agree that art, poetry, music, and other non-scientific disciplines have the potential to reveal much about human consciousness. But even if one were to deny that, it would still be important to distinguish science from non-science for the very opposite reason. I will argue that this demarcation should not involve the object of study but only the method. Without a unified concept of consciousness, a scientifically adequate explanation of what most people mean by *consciousness* is not possible. You would have different researchers explaining different things even though they all call them consciousness.

Luckily, the problem of defining consciousness may not be as big a problem as some suppose. Whatever their belief about consciousness, most people seem to have a tacit agreement regarding the concept even if they can't define it[24] and precise definitions may elude us for some time.[25] Nevertheless, I suspect that most people agree that what really needs explaining is phenomenal consciousness. If the problems requiring explanation were merely physiological or functional they would probably not be as interesting to philosophers, psychologists and others as the question of consciousness has been.[26] For that reason, Owen Flanagan's *triangulation* notion of research is very useful. Though we may originally have been interested in phenomenal consciousness, we coordinate that interest and the first person knowledge we have of it with the third person findings of neuroscience and cognitive psychology.[27] As I will attempt to show, however, this is not really sufficient and an adequate scientific treatment of consciousness will require yet other methods.

On the other side of the debate are those who attempt to reduce phenomenal consciousness to physiology or information processing. But by protesting so much they may reveal their true interests. If they were not interested in phenomenal consciousness, why would they even use the word *consciousness*? It might be better to use some neutral term without all those bad connotations. You don't see scientists re-defining ghosts, witches, or pixies.[28]

THE RELEVANCE OF PHILOSOPHY OF
THE SOCIAL SCIENCES

Consciousness is primarily a human phenomenon.[29] Many issues currently being dealt with in consciousness studies have a long history in the discussion of the nature of the human sciences. Too often, however, they are discussed without any historical orientation whatsoever and it would be helpful for students of consciousness to acquaint themselves with the predominant trends of thought in order that their current struggles can be viewed in historical perspective.

Historically, the study of humanity was associated with philosophy, but the rise of modern natural science led some to suspect that its success and methodology could be replicated in the study of humanity. The philosophy of Immanuel Kant had the overall effect of divorcing social science methodology from that prevailing methodology of the natural sciences. The Kantian notions of human freedom and history would not easily allow for a subsumption of social science under naturalistic methodology. The tendency to separate the realm of spirit from nature was accentuated even more, of course, by the followers of Hegel who emphasized spirit as an objective phenomenon. But British empiricism, perhaps best exemplified by J.S. Mill, viewed human institutions as regularities akin to those found in nature. This prompted the renewed hope that eventually universal laws of psychology would be found to explain the multifarious variety of human behaviors and institutions. Wilhelm Dilthey considered inter-subjective understanding (*Verstehen*) to be crucial to both history and social science and rejected a purely external empiricism. He believed intuitive knowledge of society and humanity is possible in contrast to the purely empirical knowledge of nature. Max Weber attempted to utilize the *Verstehen* method of Dilthey without sacrificing causal and nomological methods. His attempt to combine and reconcile those methods set the stage for subsequent work in the field. Karl Jaspers attempted to incorporate the views of Dilthey and Weber into the study of worldviews and psychopathology. This necessitated an explicitly intimate linkage between *Verstehen* and consciousness.[30]

These disputes appeared meaningless to the logical positivists and their successors who deny the distinctiveness of social science methodology in any fundamental sense. This stemmed partly from the verifiability theory of meaning that relegated non-analytic and non-empirically verifiable statements to a trash bin of emotional expression. The denial of an essential distinctiveness to social science methodology is widespread among empiricists, even those like Popper who reject logical positivism and the verifiability criterion.

Subsequent work in the philosophy and history of science has questioned the verifiability or confirmability of scientific theories; N. Goodman, K. Popper, T. Kuhn, and S. Toulmin are early examples of that trend. It is often argued nowadays that both social and natural science are interpretive, and we have surely entered an era of post-empiricism in natural science and philosophy that has not always been reflected in psychology and the other human sciences. This revolution in the general theory of science has had repercussions in the philosophy of social science, even among those schooled in the empirical and analytic traditions while continental philosophy was always uncomfortable with empiricism. Philosophers such as Taylor, MacIntyre, and Winch draw stronger distinctions between humanity and nature and between social science and natural science, while others, like Popper and Bhaskar, seek similarities.

All of the philosophical problems in social science impact heavily on the related disciplines of history and psychotherapy as well. This is particularly relevant to consciousness because of the obvious analogy between historical understanding and personal narratives. I will argue that aside from raw feelings (first person), phenomenal consciousness can be detected in others by the *Verstehen* method. Within the hermeneutic tradition, however, there is dis-agreement regarding whether understanding arises out of first per-son experiences, third person experiences of social/cultural reality, dialogical relationships (second person) or assumptions regarding rationality. I will utilize Jaspers' psychology of meaningful con-nections, which relies to a certain extent on the work of Weber, to illustrate the connection between *Verstehen* and consciousness.

MAX WEBER

Max Weber was heir to a tradition of German philosophical thought that tended to separate the world of nature from the human or social world.[31] This led to the belief that distinct methodologies were appropriate for the sciences dealing with those two categories of being, in sharp contrast to the empiricist tradition that tends to merge the two realms. Weber's attempt to reconcile those two methodologies in an uneasy coalition is well known, but in the opinion of many scholars he was not completely successful. That perception of an inadequate synthesis has led to a polarization of views, and there is even a great deal of disagreement about what he actually said and meant. It is therefore to be expected that there will continue to be controversy not only about the correctness of his views but about what his views really were. Rather than summarize Weber's views, which are certainly well known, I will simply point out two important aspects that will help make the transition to the study of consciousness.

One of the most intractable problems in the philosophy of the social sciences has been the relationship between meaningful connections and causal connections. Weber was careful to distinguish them from one another, conceptually, while insisting that they are both necessary for an adequate social science. Social acts can only be understood in terms of beliefs and expectations. *Verstehen* aims at the understanding of particular phenomena. "The type of social science in which we are interested is an empirical science of concrete reality (*wirklichkeitswissenschaft*). Our aim is the understanding of the characteristic uniqueness of the reality in which we move. We wish to understand on the one hand the relationships and the cultural significance of individual events in their contemporary manifestations and on the other the causes of their being historically so and not otherwise." (Weber, 1949, 72)

Causal and statistical analysis coexists with this understanding of concrete individuals and they are mutually dependent upon one another in social science. "Statistical uniformities constitute understandable types of action, and thus constitute sociological generalizations, only when they can be regarded as manifestations of the understandable subjective meaning of a course of social action. Conversely, formulations of a rational course of subjectively understandable action constitute sociological types of empirical process only when they can be empirically observed with a significant degree of approximation." (Weber, 1978, 12)

Perhaps Weber employed the term *Verstehen* in an ambiguous fashion, but in the introduction to *Economy and Society* he referred to Karl Jaspers' work for a fuller explication. An examination of Jaspers' *General Psychopathology* reveals *Verstehen* is a method by which a specific individual is understood in his/her uniqueness. This provides a bridge between the comprehensibility of social action and individual consciousness.[32]

KARL JASPERS' PSYCHOLOGY OF MEANINGFUL CONNECTIONS

Many of Jaspers' arguments for a *verstehende* social science overlap with the better-known work of Weber. I will concentrate on his psychology of meaningful connections, which I believe is particularly relevant to the study of consciousness. Nietzsche, Weber, Kierkegaard, and Kant were the strongest philosophical influences on Jaspers. For Jaspers, Nietzsche was the father of the psychology of meaningful connections.[33] Jaspers views this psychology as hanging precariously between empirical psychology and philosophy. It is based on an immediate intuitive insight that is analogous to the intuition that we have about causal connections.[34] Unlike causal analysis it is not generalizable, tells us nothing about whether an event will occur again but only about the *meaning* of the event. Jaspers adapted the *Verstehen* approach of Weber and Dilthey to the study of psychiatry, but in order to do that he also needed to adopt some descriptive phenomenological methods from the philosopher Edmund Husserl.

I adopted and retained Husserl's phenomenology—that he initially called "descriptive psychology"—discarding only its refinement to essence perception. It turned out to be possible and fruitful to describe the inner experiences of the sick as phenomena of consciousness. By the patient's own self-description, not only hallucinations but delusive experiences, modes of ego-consciousness and types of emotion could be defined well enough for positive recognition in other cases. Phenomenology became a research method. (Jaspers, 1986, 6)

For Jaspers, as for Dilthey, the overall state of consciousness is a self-evident feature of psychic life. But psychology must distinguish between various types of consciousness.

When speaking of individual phenomenological data, we have temporarily pre-supposed that the total state of the psyche within which these data occur remains the same; we call this the normal state of awareness and clear consciousness. But in actuality the total state of psychic life is extremely variable and the phenomenological elements are by no means always the same but have individual permutations according to what all the other elements are and to what the total state may be. . . . Traditionally this fundamental fact has been emphasized by distinguishing the *content* of consciousness . . . from the *activity of consciousness itself.* (Jaspers, 1963, 137)

Phenomenology allows him to import the *verstehende* method into the study of individuals.

Psychic events "emerge" out of each other in a way which we understand. Attacked people become angry and spring to the defense, cheated persons grow suspicious. The way in which such an emergence takes place is understood by us, our understanding is genetic. . . .

The evidence for genetic understanding is something ultimate. When Nietzsche shows how an awareness of one's weakness, wretchedness and suffering gives rise to moral demands and religions of redemption, because in this roundabout way the psyche can gratify its will to power in spite of its weakness, we experience the force of his argument and are convinced. . . . The psychology of meaningful phenomena is built up entirely on this sort of convincing experience; . . . it is not acquired inductively through repetition of experience. . . .

We can have no psychological understanding without empathy into the content (symbol, forms, images, ideas) and without seeing the expression and sharing the experienced phenomena. All these spheres of meaningful objective facts and subjective experience form the matter for understanding. Only so far as they exist can understanding take place. . . .

Thus our psychological understanding lies as it were midway between the objective facts, the phenomena of experience and the implied extra-conscious mechanisms on the one hand and the spontaneous freedom of Existence itself on the other. We might deny the object of psychological understanding altogether and maintain that phenomena, psychic contents, expression, extra-conscious mechanisms are all subjects for empirical research alone, while the possibilities of Existence itself are purely a matter for philosophy. . . . But this meaningful psychology is always in balance between these two realms and we can never speak of it in isolation . . . and if there is to be a complete presentation they cannot be separated. (Jaspers, 1963, 302–312)

Weber had described subjectively meaningful interpretations as hypotheses that had not been proven until statistical regularities could be found. But Jaspers, despite his interest in causal connections, seems to say that meaningful connections can stand on their own (to a point). Conceptually, the grasping of a meaningful connection requires no additional corroboration; but this does not render it truly scientific. As he points out, opposite interpretations are often equally meaningful and "understanding is inconclusive" because "that which is meaningful is itself inconclusive because it borders on the ununderstandable, on what is given, on human existence and on the freedom of Existence itself."[35]

But if meaningful connections are not explanations in the strictly scientific sense, what are they and where do they belong? Clearly, they are akin to philosophical insights but have a legitimate place in psychology as well. If one grants the legitimacy of this method, it becomes obvious that phenomenal consciousness exists because the entire methodology makes no sense without it.[36] For Jaspers, the human being is not just an object in the world but also pure consciousness and authentic existence (*Existenz*).

MEANINGFUL CONNECTIONS AND CAUSAL EFFICACY

Do meaningful connections have causal efficacy? This question must be distinguished from the related one regarding whether human intentions or reasons are caused by prior external events. We have seen that Jaspers separates *Verstehen* from causality and that may have been part of a desire to separate the human personality from the causal nexus, thus allowing for human freedom. There is something inherently dissatisfying in this separation however. While we like to think that our intentions are our own creations, we also like to think that they have some controlling effects on our actions and on the world and it is difficult to see how we can have it both ways.

The perennial conflict between causal connections and meaningful connections has been approached from a number of angles. Some have attempted to incorporate reasons for actions into the more scientifically respectable notion of causation. Alfred Schütz proposed converting intuitive concepts into empirically testable ones, similar to what Weber called *ideal types*, but noted the inherent limitation of the project.

> He begins to construct typical course-of-action patterns corresponding to the observed events. Thereupon he coordinates to these typical course-of-action patterns a personal type, a model of an actor whom he imagines as being gifted with consciousness. . . . Yet these models of actors are not human beings living within their biographical situation in the social world of everyday life. . . . He has created these puppets or homunculi to manipulate them for his purpose. . . . The homunculus was not born, he does not grow up, and he will not die. He has no hopes and no fears; he does not know anxiety as the chief motive of all his deeds. (Schütz, 1963, 239–40)

Others see no reason to convert reasons into causes. Peter Winch asserted that social institutions are not behavioral regularities, as J.S. Mill thought, but the conscious, voluntary adherence to social rules. "So it is quite mistaken in principle to compare the activity of a student of a form of social behavior with that of, say, an engineer studying the working of a machine. If we are going to compare the social student to an engineer, we shall do better to compare him to an apprentice engineer who is studying what engineering (that is, the activity of engineering) is all about."[37] This leads to the most radical of Winch's assertions: causal connections are out of place in the social sciences and meaningful connections are more appropriate. Insisting that Weber did not go far enough, Winch argued that most human actions are explainable by social rules and personal intention without recourse to causality.

This provoked a response by philosophers like Alasdair MacIntyre who insist meaningful connections can and do function as causes. Faulting Winch for being too much like Weber in separating reasons from causes, he also rejects another argument against meaningful connections as causes: that the relation of reasons to action is internal and conceptual rather than external and contingent. Based on an analysis of post-hypnotic suggestion, he argued: "the agent's possessing a reason may be a state of affairs identifiable independently of the event which is the agent's performance of the action. Thus it does seem as if the possession of a reason by an agent is an item of a suitable type to figure as a cause or an effect."[38] A hypnotized person may think she has a reason for doing something but empirical knowledge of hypnotism allows us to judge that she does not because her action is caused by hypnotic suggestion. That judgment is based on an assumption that if not for the hypnosis she would not perform the action and would not have had a sufficient reason for performing it. Hence having a sufficient reason is not necessarily internally constitutive of an action and may be its efficient cause.

Roy Bhaskar goes further and argues that reasons for acting must be causes at least some of the time. He argues that only if we ourselves are the cause of our actions can we be said to act and that reasons explain our actions only if they do indeed cause them.[39] Donald Davidson has also argued that reasons can only be considered truly explanatory if they are the causes of action.[40] This is relevant for those who accept the reality of consciousness but only as an emergent reality without causal efficacy since the physical universe is a closed causal system.

It seems that most contemporary thinkers are unwilling to allow meaningful connections to go it alone as the source of human agency without recourse to efficient causality, and this may be a strong intuition. Grant R. Gillett, for example, attempts to reconcile social causation and efficient causation through neural network theory.[41] Perhaps what this dispute ultimately boils down to is not whether in fact reasons can be causes (or connected to causes) in some expanded view of efficient causality. The ultimate question may be whether one can conceive of an understanding of humanity that does not involve efficient causality at all.

When Karl Popper and John Eccles collaborated on a book on this subject a difference of opinion was apparent. Popper felt that subjective mental states (World 2) have direct access to both physical (World 1) and cultural (World 3) realities. This was not a scientific theory but a kind of ontological view. Eccles, the scientist, agreed but felt (like Descartes) that he needed to pinpoint the actual physical place where World 1 and World 2 meet. This was not a problem for Popper except that it obviously could not apply to the interface between World 2 and World 3, as they are not physical. In addition, Popper suggested a statistical interpretation of the first law of thermodynamics (law of conservation of energy) in order to accommodate interaction between purely mental processes and the physical world.

Finally (perhaps to placate Eccles) Popper contemplated a quasi-revolution or "metaphysical research programme of completing physics" that would allow for interaction between the mind and the body somewhat along the lines of the interaction between the world of classical mechanics and the world of electricity. But despite the lack of any such completion of physics, Popper did not view mind-body interaction as a major philosophical problem.[42] I would argue analogously that the philosophical understanding of human behavior is not in dire need of efficient causal explanation, but that the method of *Verstehen* in the social sciences can and does benefit from an expanded view of causality.[43]

SIMULATION THEORY AND *VERSTEHEN*

Recently it has been proposed by a number of prominent thinkers that our knowledge of other minds depends not on a theory of how people think but on a kind of simulation. It is not always agreed, however, as to the nature of this simulation. It is often argued that simulation theory (ST) bears a strong similarity to the *Verstehen* method. I agree that this is the case and will briefly discuss the views of Robert Gordon and Alvin Goldman.

Gordon states that ST "bears obvious affinities to theories that particularly concern the aims and methodology of the social sciences...*Verstehen* or 'empathic understanding' and historical reenactment."[44] He then goes on to say that these "older cousins" of ST "do not enjoy the best of reputations." They have been accused of anti-naturalism and of failing to explain why an agent actually performs an act that she has a reason for performing. Gordon admits that he also subscribes to a version of anti-naturalism but that his version will function as an explanation of actions, albeit without the use of laws. He proposes as a substitute for causation and laws the use of *counterfactuals*—if we can agree that an agent would not have acted thusly if not for the reason that she had to act, that reason functions as an explanation. How does one do this? One should engage in *pretend play*—"pretend that the indicated conditions actually obtain" and then "try to make up my mind."[45] He calls this counterfactual reasoning "off line," insisting that it depends upon an assumption that the agent whose actions one is explaining is aware of her reasons and of the situation. "If I conceive the other's situation in its practical aspect, as a situation in which one is to act, then I conceive it as a situation of which the other . . . is aware."[46]

Goldman's interpretation of ST is similar, but he views the interpreter as engaging in a slightly different kind of pretense. Rather than imagining what the interpretee would think, "the interpreter tries to imagine or 'feign', the same initial states as the interpretee." and "then performs reasoning operations . . . to generate successive states in herself."[47] Goldman avoids the necessity of this operation being conscious by insisting that it is often performed automatically without a great deal of phenomenology, and it often relies on unconscious induction even though it began with conscious simulation. He calls this the "complex variant of the simulation approach"[48]

I have no problem with either of these interpretations, but simulation might seem to require some kind of awareness by the interpretee that *Verstehen* does not in principle require. Jaspers, for example, discussed Nietzsche's view that ethical and redemptive religion is a means by which the wretched exert power over others who are more powerful. Does that mean that the powerless consciously adopt such religiosity for that purpose? Obviously not! Perhaps there are unconscious mental processes involved. It is true that we rely upon such connections to predict behavior because (presumably) they have proven useful and reliable more often than not.

Goldman sees that but insists such quasi-inductive inference be based on initial simulations. But considering the example from Jaspers, the logical scheme by which such "reasons" imply beliefs or actions is far from apparent. Even if we accept unconscious ideation and assume that a group has a will to power but is relatively powerless, can we infer redemptive religion will be the result? My point is that *Verstehen* also deals with meaningful connections that would be very difficult to simulate without extraordinary insight.[49] I agree therefore with Theodore Schatzki that "simulation theory can at best be one of several pillars of a defense of the *verstehende* tradition."[50]

CONSCIOUSNESS AND THE NATURE OF SCIENTIFIC REASONING

If there is indeed a conflict between the view of the human being provided by physics and chemistry and that provided by comprehensive theories in social science, how does one go about resolving it? Despite a lively phenomenological opposition, the prevailing trend in consciousness studies seems to resolve it in favor of the naturalistic worldview. We see this bias even in the case of many thinkers who employ theories of social or cultural causation as well as in those who espouse neutral monism. They often attempt to justify their theories by harmonizing them with physicalist models.

It is perfectly understandable that scientists (whether they be physicists, psychologists or biologists) will attempt to approach this problem using the paradigm that is available to them from their training and experience. Nevertheless, they can perhaps come to recognize that there are other legitimate approaches to the same problem. Thomas Natsoulas, who has written extensively regarding the many meanings of *consciousness*, denies that there "is a right way to do science," and argues that psychology would benefit much more if it would "tolerate other perspectives." He goes on to suggest that: "We should do what we can to nurture them."[51]

I would add that it would be a major advance if psychologists would come to accept the fact that radically different approaches in science do not necessarily constitute an intolerable contradiction. This may appear to be a controversial statement since science is so often associated with rationality and most people do not believe in radically different rationalities. But science is not a geometric system of axioms, postulates, etc. within which each true proposition logically follows from more basic ones, though it may look like that at times. In science we follow traditions and within those traditions we sometimes make bold conjectures. But no matter how traditional or innovative we may be, the certainty with which we hold to scientific positions is not generally the same kind of certainty that we might possess regarding other matters, and the proof of that is our ability to use irreconcilable theoretical orientations.

If I am truly certain of a proposition, I should be equally certain of every proposition that is logically entailed by it but such a stance would destroy science, as we know it. I am referring to the fact that every scientific theory looks like an ontology in conflict with other ontologies but really is not. If you really are ontologically certain that light consists of particles, then it can't possibly consist of waves. If you are really certain of economic theory as the essentially correct way to explain human behavior, then you must reject competing theories in anthropology, sociology, psychology, etc.

I will grant that within each specific discipline, and even more so within each particular theoretical orientation, every effort is made to root out inconsistencies. This has been especially true of the physical sciences where no large disputes existed regarding causality, agency, etc. It may become less true in those sciences as they continue the exploration of levels of physical reality where particles don't look or act like physical things. Be that as it may, most of us use apparently conflicting scientific disciplines and theories and most scientists see no problem with this.

One explanation for this is that such theoretical scientific certainty as we possess is only a methodological device allowing us to deduce consequences (some of which eventually falsify the very theory that we were previously certain of). Although incongruities in our scientific worldviews may induce us to accept a competing theory, we should not lose sight of the fact that scientific theories are basically conjectural and subject to revision. If I was once certain of a scientific theory and it was eventually proven to be false, I don't have to ask myself why I was so sure of that theory and question every step in the process that originally led me to believe in it. I simply admit that a conjecture that seemed right has turned out to be wrong.

True conviction regarding reality can at times arise out of scientific knowledge, but the fact that some physicists have been idealists and others realists should dispel the notion that hard science *necessarily* leads to ontological certainty. Some scientists and philosophers of science, of course, are quite certain regarding ontological or metaphysical matters. As Rom Harré has pointed out, the universality and necessity of natural laws are survivors from a religious past and require interpretation.[52] But not everyone interprets them in a realist fashion.

Charles Varela approvingly attributes the following position to Harré: "scientific theory is a disguised metaphysic (a 'type hierarchy') of the beings of a world for a given domain of interest."[53] But this seems more to me like a provisional lower ontology than a full-blown metaphysics. If metaphysical certainty were a *general* requirement for them, scientists might be as divided and contentious as are metaphysicians and this simply is not the case—except in the social sciences. There, perhaps, Varela and Harré may be quite correct regarding the need for metaphysics, and it may stem from those sciences' need for understanding (*Verstehen*).[54]

Even in the social sciences, however, one should not ground one's metaphysics on current knowledge. Bhaskar terms that the "epistemic fallacy . . . the view that statements about being can be reduced to or analyzed in terms of statements about knowledge."[55] Since the views of reality of the specialized sciences are not always the same, we have to live with some inconsistencies. This should prevent us from taking any partial view to its logical conclusion even though the tendency to reconcile all contrary notions about reality remains strong. Hence the quasi-materialist proposition that only physical and related entities such as fields or waves are real seems appropriate in natural science but not in the social sciences and certainly not in our daily lives. If this argument is accepted, there is no need to deny phenomenal consciousness simply because it is not part of the worldview of natural science. On the contrary, the belief in phenomenal consciousness may well be a cornerstone of economics, sociology, and other human sciences.

CONCLUSION

The scientific study of consciousness can learn a great deal from prior debates in the social sciences and particularly from the *verstehende* method. On the one hand, we need to take the causal and nomological methods of natural science seriously (even though they don't take as their object phenomenal consciousness) since the ontology appropriate to natural science is physical monism. But we also need to recognize the relationship between consciousness and the inter-subjective grasping of meaningful connections. That relationship operates on the level of meaning, which cannot be supported by a physicalist ontology. Any attempt to squeeze the human sciences into such an ontology results in an impoverished methodology. Hence we are drawn to a dualist (or pluralist) epistemology, which in turn suggests a dualistic or pluralistic ontology. The difficult task is finding a way to reconcile the radically different approaches that pertain to the natural and human sciences.

Some have conjectured that we will never solve this problem unless and until we expand our concept of causality.[56] That may well be true, but until that happens we would be well advised to recognize phenomenal consciousness as a given, which can mostly be known in a non-scientific manner via first person reports. Science is not the only source of knowledge and much knowledge of phenomenal consciousness may never be scientific. If, by analogy, we confined the study of art to the various scientific disciplines, our aesthetic knowledge would be greatly impoverished.

But aside from the importance of the humanities, it must also be recognized that the *verstehende* methods of the social sciences can indeed study phenomenal consciousness scientifically. It does this in a variety of ways, many of which we are only dimly aware of. Such methods may utilize first-person phenomenological reports as starting points or they may not, but they also require an inter-subjective consensus in order to give them true scientific status.[57]

NOTES

1. See Damasio, 1994, 250–52.
2. He even blames Descartes for artificial intelligence and other types of cognitive science not usually considered dualist in nature. See ibid., 250–51.
3. Ibid., 89.
4. See Descartes, 1989, article 51.
5. Goldman gives this as a first approximation of a definition of functionalism. "the reportability or accessibility of a mental state is part of what it means for such a state to be conscious" (Goldman, 2000, 7). It seems to me that functionalism is generally a sort of epiphenomenalism as long as one's ontology is still physicalist.
6. See Ghaemi, 2003, 26, where he views it as a promising viewpoint within a pluralistic psychiatric methodology.
7. For Searle (1992, 90) consciousness is "a biological feature of human and certain animal brains." Depending upon how he uses the word *is*, he might have to admit that this "biological feature" could conceivably be a feature of

machinery as well. He gives a hint of why he cannot conceive of such a thing. On the same page he states that beliefs in God or an afterlife are not simply lacking in any good evidence but are contrary to our worldview and that this worldview is "not an option," not "up for grabs" but something peculiarly compelling. Most people who reject the possibility of machines being conscious probably don't feel so strongly about this "worldview" as does Searle. One could of course argue that it is perfectly rational to be skeptical about conjoined events that have never been perceived in all of human history, and that this is the reason why most people reject the idea of conscious machines. Burge's position seems to me much closer to how we really conceptualize consciousness. He distinguishes phenomenal qualities from phenomenal consciousness itself, which is not only phenomenal but also affective. This seems right and, if so, machines are excluded due to lack of an affective element. See Burge (1998).

8. See Natsoulas, 1978.

9. See Guzeldere, 1996.

10. It has also been argued, for example by Bhaskar (1998) that physicalist models don't explain the natural world very well either, but that is beyond the scope of this study. I assume that physicalist models do a good job in the physical sciences even if they are not metaphysically satisfying.

11. My use of the term *naturalism* is consistent with that of Popper and others. For a good discussion, see Keat, 1971. The denial of naturalism is a radical claim because it is often assumed that coherence with naturalism lends credence to *any* science. And in fact, that assumption, coupled with a Humean view of external reality and laws of nature, was once quite attractive to this author. Nevertheless, I have come to reject it. On the other hand, my claim has nothing to do with the supernatural. It simply asserts that naturalism does not exhaust the possibilities of knowledge of humanity. Some might infer from this assertion that there is an aspect of humanity completely beyond nature, but others might conclude that it is an emergent property not requiring anything supernatural. I argue that this is irrelevant to social science, which does not obtain legitimacy by being understandable in terms of natural science but by explaining human thought, behavior, artifacts, culture, social processes, etc. To insist that these be comprehensible in terms of some preconceived view of the "natural" is to limit their investigation. In fact, the study of humanity pre-dates the current concept of nature (if there is such a concept). I am not suggesting, however, that a reasonable account of human behavior can contradict the findings of natural science.

12. See Rakover, 1992, 148.

13. Joseph Margolis (1974) argues that both physicalists and functionalists are guilty of this, either by identifying consciousness with a part of the

physical system or with states of information processing ascribed to parts of the nervous system.

14. There are many interesting articles that touch upon it. See the *Verstehen* article by Philip Petit (1987, 786–87). The writings of Alvin Goldman deal with it extensively. Another thinker who closely approximates my own views is A.J. Marcel. See Marcel, 1992, and see Oatley, 1992. Tom Burns has written specifically on the connection between sociology and consciousness but the article that I reviewed does not deal extensively with the philosophical underpinnings of social science or the psychology of meaningful connections; it focuses on collective processes. See Burns and Engdahl, 1998. Francisco Varela's neurophenomenological approach (Varela, 1998) is obviously relevant, but I intend to discuss a less specific approach within the phenomenological tradition. D.R. Watson (1998) has written an article on ethnomethodology which runs parallel to many of my concerns but stresses somewhat different areas of social science. A most interesting book has appeared relating *Verstehen* to simulation theory. I have attempted to incorporate many of its insights. See Kogler and Stueber, 2000.

15. See K. Wilkes, 1993.

16. This is obviously an attractive proposition for those who would like to deny phenomenal consciousness. If you can show that a rational sophisticated culture can get along just fine without such a concept, it takes you quite a way toward your goal. But, interestingly, the point has also been made by some who do believe in phenomenal consciousness. For example, Hamlyn (1963, xiii) sees in Aristotle's failure to note a mind-body problem an inadequacy in the Aristotelian concept of the soul. See Hamlyn. I believe that there are two distinct problems here. The first problem is the relative strangeness of ancient Greek civilization. The second problem has to do with what kind of concept phenomenal consciousness is. Is it so absolutely indispensable that no culture could function without it? I tend to think that there are many concepts that can be well defended without insisting upon that as a criterion. There are often things so obvious and close to us that we don't look at them carefully. The history of rational thought has involved the bringing to light of problems that were implicit in previous ways of thinking but that had not heretofore been examined.

17. There is already a tension in Plato between the soul as the reasonable aspect of the person or as comprising rational and irrational elements. Later on, this became crystallized in the Aristotelian tradition in the concepts of vegetable, animal, and rational souls. Aside (perhaps) from some of the Arabic thinkers such as al Kindi, Descartes was the first major thinker to clearly define the soul as purely rational and therefore to reject those other kinds of souls.

18. Ironically, this is denied by many scholars who feel bewildered by the stark religiosity of the medievals and imagine that they would have felt more comfortable in ancient Greece. I should hope that my earlier discussions would have disabused some of that prejudice, but for those who are not yet convinced, I recommend a reading of Burckhardt (1998).

19. This might explain its popularity among philosophers of social science.

20. In my view of the relationship between ontology and scientific theory I generally follow Popper and reject the overall claim of realists such as Bhaskar. Nevertheless, I also think that there are aspects of the human sciences where the distinction between ontology and theory breaks down completely. Consciousness may be one of them.

21. See Harré and Madden, 1975; Greenwood, 1988; and Bhaskar, 1998.

22. Different people have different views on what that gap is, but basically it is a gap between our means of scientifically detecting consciousness (third person accounts) and what the word *consciousness* really means. Perhaps it would be better to call it a gap in understanding.

23. Such powers can underwrite a non-deterministic kind of causality. The term *conversational realism* was used by Charles A. Varela and Rom Harré to describe the power of people to manage symbols that brings about social order. They accuse Bhaskar of neglecting this in favor of transcendental social structures. The rejection of actualism and the determinism that attends it gives rise to the alternative concept of causal powers which "underwrites the thesis of conversational realism . . . or the thesis of transcendental social structures. . . . But it cannot underwrite both." (Varela and Harré, 1996, 316).

24. "Everyone has a rough idea of what is meant by consciousness." (Crick and Koch, 1997, 278).

25. "Definitions and precise theoretical constructs are the final product, not the starting point of enquiry." (Weiskrantz, 1992, 183). According to Dilthey, phenomenal consciousness is such a fundamental datum that it can't be defined or analyzed. He contrasts it with its derivative representational awareness which has been the subject of epistemological disputes. See Dilthey, 1989, 25.

26. On this issue, I both agree and disagree with David Galin. He argues that there is little agreement regarding what needs to be studied, but he also argues that "what is most interesting about mental life for most ordinary people is not mechanism, not performance, not information processing; it is what it feels like!" (Galin, 1996, 121). I argue that no matter what some researchers *think* they are studying, their real motivation is to explain phenomenal consciousness. Since we don't find phenomenal consciousness without functional consciousness, whenever we study the latter, we hope to learn something about the former. But some say it is possible that the func-

tional consciousness can exist in humans without phenomenality—i.e., in zombies).

27. See Flanagan, 1992. Alvin Goldman points out some very interesting uses for Flanagan's model. For example, when we can't know whether the person was unconscious or was conscious for a brief instant and then forgot, neuroscience could help to decide (Goldman, 1997). One could think of many other uses. For example, one could dispute first-person accounts on the basis of either psychological evidence or brain science, and the latter may also give us a clue into whether or not other species possess phenomenal consciousness.

28. That is not to say that social scientists don't take an interest in illusions and delusions. Obviously they take a great interest in belief systems that they take to be false, but they rarely attempt to re-define the terms in such a way that the beliefs become true. An important exception that may bear more than an accidental similarity to our subject is religion. Many students of religion attempt to reinterpret religious beliefs to refer to social rather than supernatural phenomena.

29. I recognize that most if not all researchers believe that consciousness exists in the animal world. But such consciousness is rudimentary in comparison to the human variety and perhaps should not even be given the same name. It must be allowed, however, that the admission of animal consciousness militates against Cartesian dualism and lends support to neutral monism or panpsychism.

30. Ron Levine (1977, 240) also argues that the human "second–order monitoring capacity" is the basis for an interpretive or *Verstehen* social science. That second–order monitoring capacity turns out to be consciousness: "man's ability to be not only aware of his environment like other animals, but aware of being aware."

31. Talcott Parsons attributed it to Kant's notion of the world of "spirit" in his introduction to Weber (1969, 8–10).

32. For a contemporary sympathetic reappraisal of Jaspers' work in psychiatry, see S. Nassir Ghaemi, 2003.

33.This in itself serves to distinguish it from other types of *Verstehen*. It is interesting that many have also viewed psychoanalysis as related to Nietzsche. Jaspers' attitude toward psychoanalysis was ambivalent and not altogether favorable. He viewed it as a psychology of meaningful connections that offers itself as a causal explanation.

34. This intuition is probably what we would now call realist rather than Humean. Hume's view of causality seems to deny that intuition is telling us anything about reality.

35. See Jaspers, 1963, 357.

36. This raises the question as to whether consciousness might be regarded as a theoretical fiction within the framework of social science. It is certainly a logical possibility, but most people would believe strongly in the existence of that which is intuitively certain and also useful as a scientific explanatory device.

37. See Winch, 1958, 88.

38. See MacIntyre, 1982, 297.

39. See Bhaskar, 1998, 80–97.

40. See Davidson, 1963. Many of these disputes, interesting as they may be, revolve around the notions of explanation and causality. These are such primitive and essential notions that it is difficult to believe that there could be any respectable explication aside from them, or that they could be anything but synonymous. Aristotle, of course, posited four kinds of causality, efficient causality being only one of them. Those who separate meaningful connections from causal connections generally refer only to efficient causation. The distinction between explanation and understanding does not necessarily deny that the latter has an explicatory function. Nor does it deny that the understanding of human events requires a broader concept of causality. Clearly, however, such an expanded concept would include necessary conditions and would not be restricted to sufficient conditions.

41. See Gillett, 1993, 27.

42. The dialogue between them will be more fully discussed in the appendix to this book. See Popper and Eccles, 1977, Dialogue 10.

43. For a good discussion of alternative causal views, see Greenwood, 1988. It may be that something like Popper's propensity theory of probability could support a causal theory that allows for human freedom. This has been suggested by Malcolm Williams, 1999, and previously by this author in an unpublished doctoral dissertation, 1997.

44. See Kogler and Stueber, 2000, 62.

45. See ibid., 77.

46. See ibid., 79.

47. See Goldman, 1992, 21.

48. See ibid., 24.

49. See Kogler and Stueber (2000, 40–42) for a discussion of the limits of hermeneutical interpretation that does not take into consideration such factors as ideology, social class, and psychopathology—all of which influence consciousness, but regarding which the subject is often unaware.

50. See ibid., 179.

51. See Natsoulas, 1992, 200–01.

52. See Harré, 1993, 10.

53. See Varela, 1999, 393.

54. If my suspicion is correct, the need for metaphysical certainty in science has been misplaced from the human sciences (where it is most urgently needed) to the natural sciences (that can do quite well without it because of their palpable and practical results, which give them a quite sufficient *raison d' être*).

55. See Bhaskar, 1978, 36.

56. The problem here is essentially the same as the one encountered on the subatomic level where existing models of causality don't apply. Nevertheless, that does not prevent researchers in quantum mechanics from reporting their findings.

57. Exactly how this is to be achieved is not yet universally agreed upon, as it is in some other sciences. Nevertheless, we do have a fairly good example of agreement in economics, and less agreed upon rules in the other social sciences.

Chapter Seven

Damasio, James, and Jaspers on Emotion

Antonio Damasio states: "The contents of feelings are the configurations of body state represented in somatosensing maps."[1] He repeats such statements again and again, and his view of emotions relies heavily upon a theory independently developed by William James and Carl Georg Lange, commonly known as the James-Lange theory. He commends it many times in *Looking for Spinoza* as if it were a generally accepted theory.

William James devotes a chapter in his *Principles of Psychology* to emotion and he relies to a great extent upon Lange, a Danish physiologist. They believe that emotions are strongly related to instincts but are more extensive since the instincts have external practical foci whereas emotions often do not. James expresses his theory as follows: My theory . . . is that *the bodily changes follow directly the perception of the exciting fact, and that our feeling of the same changes as they occur is the emotion.*"[2]

He justifies the theory in the following ways. Firstly, no one should deny or doubt that "*objects do excite bodily changes* by a preorganized mechanism, or the farther fact that *the changes are so indefinitely numerous and subtle that the entire organism may be called a sounding-board*, which every change of consciousness, however slight, may make reverberate."[3] Secondly, "*every one of the bodily changes, whatsoever it be, is* FELT, *acutely or obscurely, the moment it occurs.*"[4] Finally, the "vital point" of the theory is as follows. "*If we fancy some strong emotion, and then try to abstract from our consciousness of it all the feelings of its bodily symptoms, we find we have nothing left behind,* no 'mind-stuff' out of which the emotion can be constituted, and that a cold and neutral state of intellectual perception is all that remains."[5]

He admits immediately, however, that not all people agree that their "introspection verifies this statement." He also admits that his theory is only a causal one and does not affect the phenomenological data. "But our emotions must always be *inwardly* what they are, whatever be the physiological ground of their apparition."[6] The theory allows for what James calls causal questions and a "deep order of inquiry."[7]

The raw data, both phenomenological and empirical, do show a strong relationship between bodily states and emotional states. The traditional view of course is that emotional states cause the body to do certain things. When an animal is afraid it tends to run away or tremble. The fear (emotion) is often conceptualized as causing the behavior or action. But James argued that it is the bodily state that causes the fear. He hypothesized an initial cold cortical response to stimuli followed by an emotionally colored response once the peripheral somatic changes are reported to the cerebral cortex.

James thought his theory could probably never be proven or refuted but various experimenters have found reasons for accepting or rejecting it. It does seem to accord with our common experiences to a certain extent. For example, I have noticed that when my horse is initially spooked by something, it begins to run away and then after a few seconds it may or may not begin to panic. If you can keep the horse still, it tends not to panic further but woe to the rider who cannot control the horse's impulse to flee. This may be a result of somatic feedback, including feedback from the rider's response.

But the contextual reason for the initial response is also significant. If it is initially spooked by a deer or bird, it realizes almost immediately that there is nothing to fear and does not panic. But if the object that initially caused it to run is something less familiar (perhaps a school bus or the smell of a bear) it may begin to panic shortly after the initial flight response. So I would argue (and many psychologists would agree) that the initial behavioral response (flight) and the initial stimulus are each a factor causing an emotional response as are other factors such as objects in the environment and/or internal ideas. Indeed, the very concept of running away is contextual because animals run when they are not afraid and often appear to be experiencing very positive emotions while running. Now, with the horse, we would say that a large, noisy unfamiliar object (school bus) tends to induce fear just as does one that it may be instinctually averse to (a bear).

With people there are unfamiliar frightful objects and those that we may be genetically averse to (snakes), and there are also things that we are culturally averse to or psychologically averse to as individuals. All those things color our emotional responses, including the perception of our bodily processes. Some psychologists favor this kind of a feedback loop theory that includes perception of visceral responses as only one factor.

A great many other objections to the James-Lange theory have been raised. I will only mention a few of them. Patients whose spinal cords have been severed still report emotions, albeit many report duller ones. Many theorists believe the James-Lange theory is untenable because it implies too long a time delay. Visceral responses to various stimuli may not vary enough in order to account for all emotional nuances. In addition, all perception may be emotionally colored because of previous experience, something that James seemed to believe. Nevertheless, the James-Lange theory may explain some emotional reactions if not all.

Damasio distinguishes between emotional states of the organism and feelings, which are perceptions of those bodily states. But is it true, as Damasio claims, that feelings are simply perceptions of our bodily processes? He must be aware of the experimental controversies regarding the James-Lange theory, yet he appears to accept it wholeheartedly. I suspect that he views it more as a metaphysical assertion than as a scientific hypothesis that can be tested empirically. I am pleased, however, that he equates feelings with perceptions because he might have made the even larger error of equating feelings with the bodily processes themselves. He insists that feelings are mental events. But what are *mental events*?

As I have repeated many times in this study, what really needs explaining (or understanding) in consciousness is *experience*. We also saw, in Chapter Three, that Damasio fails to effectively deal with that issue, which includes the experience of emotion (the feeling). We need to look not only at empirical data to understand what a feeling state is but we also need to look at the phenomenological aspect. Setting metaphysics aside for now, how can we even begin to understand emotions without asking the question: What does it feel like? And Damasio's theory, by explaining feelings away too easily, prevents or at least dissuades us from doing that. We would do well to return to a very different approach and one that both allows for and encourages empirical research. Let us begin that phenomenological exploration by inspecting, once again, Karl Jaspers' *General Psychopathology*.

Jaspers distinguishes between the content of consciousness and the activity of consciousness itself. In other words, we can inspect the phenomenological data and assume that the overall state of the psyche always remains the same but that is only a useful methodology in order to restrict our view to one thing at a time. In reality, the overall psyche is also changing.[8] Therefore, emotions or feelings must also be inspected in the modes in which they appear. The following are excerpts of how Jaspers categorizes feelings phenomenologically.

Feelings can color object awareness, as in the James-Lange theory, but they can also be aspects of the conscious personality. Hence we can speak of a fearful person as *objectless* or *contentless* (experiencing anxiety), or as *directed to an object* (experiencing fear). Some feelings can be directed onto suppositions and others onto real objects. Some feelings are localized *feeling-sensations*; others regard the entire body. There are *psychic* feelings like sadness and joy. There are *spiritual* feelings like the state of grace. Feelings can be categorized in terms of their biological purpose. Pleasurable feelings express *advancement* of those purposes and unpleasurable ones express *frustration*. Particular feelings must be distinguished from all-inclusive ones that are called *feeling-states.*

Feelings are "states of the self"; sensations are "elements of perception of the environment or of one's body." For example, one can be suffering without experiencing physical pain. Some feeling-sensations are both—e.g., hunger, thirst, fatigue and sexual excitement.

Abnormal feeling-states fall into two categories. The first "emerge in understandable fashion from some experience." The second "defeat understanding" and must be attributed to some unconscious factors.

The following are further ways of categorizing emotions or feelings:

(1) Bodily feelings are "always associated with emotion." But in some abnormal states that connection becomes "strange and difficult to comprehend."

(2) We ordinarily are "confident" regarding our capacities. But this can change to "feelings of insufficiency."

(3) Patients can have flat affect (apathy). In extreme cases they have "no emotion whatsoever and he/she would die if not for external intervention."

(4) Unlike apathy, patients can also have an "unpleasant" recognition that they have no emotions.

(5) Sometimes ordinary experiences and perceptions become unpleasant.

(6) Some feelings are unattached (free-floating). Examples are free-floating anxiety, anxiety linked with restlessness, abnormal feelings of happiness or mystical ecstasy.

(7) Private worlds can grow out of unattached feelings. This can also occur as a result of epileptic auras or drug-induced experiences. They often take on a religious or spiritual character.[9]

Aside from those ways of viewing emotions, it is also important to see how emotions might affect other aspects of consciousness. They can, for example, take over the normal field of consciousness.

> When there are *violent affects*, as in anxiety states and deep melancholia as well as in manic states, it becomes much more difficult to concentrate on anything external, contemplate anything, reach a judgment, or even think of anything. . . . For this reason . . . the contents of delusion-like ideas go unscrutinised by the patient. . . . Consciousness is completely filled by the affect, and judgment and attitude become very disturbed in an understandable way. This is even more the case in depressive states . . . which may become a persisting emptiness of consciousness in the last named instance. (Jaspers, 1963, 14)

CONCLUSION

Damasio focuses primarily on the linkage between feelings/emotions and physiological changes. He justifies this by following the James-Lange theory of emotion but fails to be critical enough of it as a scientific theory. This is one more example of his basic metaphysical predilection. Unfortunately, this prevents a thorough treatment of feelings from the phenomenological perspective. Therefore, linking feelings and emotions only to physiological responses is a diminution of the richness of human psychic experience and can only lead to an impoverished metaphysics.

Jaspers' treatment of emotion links those states with physiology on one side and with worldviews on the other. Emotional states condition one's worldview and one's worldview conditions one's emotional states. Worldviews contain volitional elements that color one's entire psychic life. Only by suspending metaphysical judgments (at least temporarily) can we achieve a rich phenomenological description. That is because metaphysical assertions almost inevitably affect our beliefs regarding which experiences are significant and which are not.

NOTES

1. Damasio, 2003, 132.
2. James, 1981, 1065.
3. Ibid., 1066.

4. Ibid.
5. Ibid., 1067.
6. Ibid., 1068.
7. Ibid., 1069.
8. See Jaspers, 1963, 137.
9. For his treatment of emotions and consciousness, see Jaspers, 1963, 108–27.

Appendix

Karl Popper's Three Worlds in the Study of Mind and Consciousness

The relevance of the Three Worlds model to the philosophy of mind, neuroscience, and the study of consciousness should require little in the way of justification since they were motivating factors in the creation of the model. In my view, its application to consciousness may have implications in a multitude of sub-specialties of the human sciences despite the fact that Popper himself never developed a distinct philosophy of the social sciences. But if one were to accept the model, I see no reason why one cannot confine any particular science to one or two of the three worlds and this would seem to support my call for a pluralistic methodology and ontology.

Popper began to discuss this subject in great detail in his Emory lectures of 1969 and they have more recently been published.[1] World 1 is the all too familiar physical world. World 2 is the world of human consciousness or mental activity. World 3 is objective culture, which is the creation of World 2 but takes on its own distinct and permanent existence. Popper took no position regarding the ultimate origin of the three worlds but assumed that

World 2 and World 3 emerge out of World 1. Hence, this theory may be more palatable to materialists than some of the others that we have discussed.

The best known work in which Popper promoted his views regarding consciousness is his collaborative effort with the neurophysiologist Sir John Eccles entitled *The Self and its Brain.* Eccles was both a scientist and a religious believer. Popper was neither, though he was, of course, one of the most prominent philosophers of science of the twentieth century. The arguments in that book are extremely wide-ranging and it is clear that Popper and Eccles are not always in complete agreement, no matter how hard they attempt to reach a consensus in the third section that is devoted to dialogue. This makes the work even more valuable and it seems to me that this book is still one of our greatest resources in this area of inquiry. Three years before that book was published, Popper also engaged in some rather interesting arguments on this and other subjects with a number of modern thinkers (including Eccles), many of which have been published in *The Philosophy of Karl Popper.*

DISPUTES REGARDING THE THREE WORLDS

One very interesting dispute between Popper and Eccles regards the precise meaning of World 3. That dispute first emerged in *The Philosophy of Karl Popper.* Eccles, of course, is in general agreement regarding the three worlds. But he asks why one cannot consider long-term neural potentiation (long-term memory) to be part of World 3 just like a book or a computer file. Popper responds that it is not the book (as a physical thing) that is part of World 3 but the cultural content or meaning of the book. The same could be said of memory, of course, and Eccles insists that long-term, reproducible memory can also convey World 3 information. What is the difficulty here?

This dispute surfaced again in the dialogue section of *The Self and Its Brain* and it seems to involve Eccles' desire to view all interaction between the three worlds as a kind of causal interaction while Popper seems to envision some non-causal interaction between World 3 and World 2.

Eccles: I agree completely with the statement that there must be causal openness of World 1 towards World 2, but I rather feel that a misunderstanding can arise if we speak about the causal openness of World 2 to World 3 by direct action. I would like to suggest that in between there is always inserted a step via World 1.

Popper: I would suggest that instead of saying that World 3 is encoded in the brain, we say that certain World 3 objects are recorded in the brain and thus, as it were, incarnated. The whole of World 3 is nowhere; it is only certain individual World 3 objects which are sometimes incarnated and thus localized.[2]

One certainly gets the impression that the two authors are talking past one another. Since both World 2 and World 3 are immaterial, Popper sees no reason why there cannot be direct interaction without causality (at least of the ordinary kind). Eccles, as one trained in scientific methodology and attempting to render the view more scientific, wants to find some "liaison brain" where the three worlds meet. Given these seemingly irreconcilable perspectives, it is quite remarkable that they do reach some sort of agreement. This occurs in a later dialogue after a discussion of Euclid's solution of the problem of the greatest prime number, which was accomplished by visualizing an infinite series.

Popper: Let me illustrate this by discussing Euclid's theorem, that for every natural number, however large, there exists a greater one which is a prime number; or in other words, that there are infinitely many primes. . . . The solution of the problem is that, if we assume that there is a greatest prime number, then with the help of this alleged "greatest prime number" *we can construct a greater one*. . . . There is something going on in World 1, but this process of grasping goes beyond what is going on in World 1; and this may perhaps be a reason to suppose that it is really the Wernicke centre which contains some open modules; an opening of World 1 to World 2.

Eccles: Yes, I am convinced that the Euclidean story indicates a direct relationship between World 3 and World 2. Now that I have fully understood it, it is very convincing indeed. . . . As a World 2-World 3 interaction, it is happening independently of the brain and then gets coded back on the brain.[3]

Despite the fact that Eccles now accepts a non-causal kind of relationship between World 3 and World 2 and begins to view it as a kind of self-exploration, there is still a problem. Self-exploration by the mind, as a means of creative activity, still seems to presuppose a prior relationship between the mind and World 3. Once this mysterious creative activity takes place, Eccles still insists that the results must be encoded onto the brain. But there is also a problem in that view in terms of the objectivity of World 3. Every reading of a book is different just as every arousal of memory is different: they are both re-constructions. The book appears to have an objective core, however, because we can make meaningful statements about different people's reading of the same book. The objective core that we consider crucial here is not the physical material of which the book is constructed, but the language, and even more so the ideas or concepts which the language conveys.

Long-term memory also has an objective core in terms of neuronal connections but there does not seem to be something analogous to objectively available language and ideas because memory can only be read by one person. So there is a problem with Eccles' view and perhaps one *does* need public access before it is fruitful to refer to World 3.

On the other hand, this also raises some difficulties regarding Popper's insistence that World 3 is *nowhere*, because objectivity seems to require something *somewhere* that one can point to. If the memory expresses itself in an oral tradition, for example, one would have a genuine World 3 object. Until that happens, long-term memory is something that resembles World 3, leads to it and is probably as close to it as one can get, but does not yet qualify unless there were some independent public means of reproducing it.

This also applies to creativity; a creative act does not really seem to be a part of World 3 until a proof or at least some criterion of acceptability is publicly available. For example, oral traditions existed for thousands of years, were encoded in long-term memory, and were certainly part of World 3, but since they were recited from time to time and accepted by communities, they were never the possession of only one person. Without this criterion of public acceptability, one might have to admit that a nonsense rhyme created and memorized by a child is as much a part of World 3 as the poems of Wordsworth.[4]

Nevertheless, long-term memory is a very problematic area in neuroscience and the linkage with culture is obvious and may yet bear fruit. It is obvious, for example, that things tend to go into long-term memory when they are meaningful. If everyone's schedule of meaning were utterly unique, it would be pretty difficult to teach a class or motivate a workforce. So despite the difficulties, long-term memory does seem to be closely related to World 3. Those difficulties, of course, could perhaps be resolved if we were able to find some inherent linkage between World 1 and World 3 but that might require a more religious perspective than Popper was willing to adopt.

Mario Bunge and Ruben Ardilla have written a fairly comprehensive book, from an empiricist perspective, entitled *Philosophy of Psychology*. They exhibit a particular animus against the dualist interactionist perspective of Popper and Eccles and detail eight separate objections to it. It would be difficult to find a more comprehensive critique.

First, it is half-baked because its key concepts—notably those of world, mind and interaction—are undefined and it does not contain any precise hypotheses about the nature of mind or its alleged interaction with the brain. Second, it violates "a fundamental tenet of physics," namely the principle of conservation of energy (because it postulates that immaterial mind can move matter). Third, it violates a tacit assumption of all experimental science, namely that the mind cannot act directly upon matter—for, if it could, no instrument reading would be worth anything. Fourth, it assumes that mental states and processes are unlike any other states and processes, in that they are not states of things or processes in things—whence it perpetuates the ontological anomaly of classical psychology. Fifth, it is inconsistent with the tacit presupposition underlying physiological psychology, namely that mental states are brain states. Sixth, it is inconsistent with evolutionary biology, which acknowledges only material things. Seventh, the doctrine calls for a bit of parapsychology, namely the conjecture that the mind is to the brain as the performer is to the piano keyboard (Eccles' metaphor). Eighth, although the doctrine fits in nicely with mainstream Christian theology, it has been used to accuse materialists of dogmatism and even of confusing their science with their religion.[5]

As to the first complaint: it is impossible to define all of one's terms because eventually one encounters circularity or an infinite regress. It is as true now as it was when Aristotle first enunciated the principle that scientific theories rest on more basic principles, which are obtained intuitively (or simply postulated as is often the case with modern science). Perhaps the interactionist view could profit from better defining of its terms if it wants to compete as a psychological theory, but it should be clear by now that it is basically a metaphysical theory, which it is hoped will lead to fruitful scientific discoveries.

The second objection regarding the law of conservation of energy is a substantial one. Indeed, Popper anticipated such an objection.

One possibility that would suit us extremely well would be that the law of the conservation of energy would turn out to be valid only statistically. . . . In fact, some physicists have proposed theories in which the conservation of energy is only statistically valid. . . .

In other words, modern physics is pluralistic (and the law of conservation of energy had constantly to be generalized whenever the physical world was enlarged). Thus, we should not be too worried about a *prima facie* violation of this law: somehow we may be able to work it out.[6]

Eccles also has a reply to this anticipated objection.

In my discussions with Eugene Wigner, I get the impression that he feels a complete transformation of physics is required, not just an addition to some aspect of physical law but that the very basis of physics has to be reconstructed with a revolution that would transform the existing physics more than occurred with the earlier physics under the influence of Einsteinian relativity and Planck's quantum theory.[7]

And he gives another argument, which is even more persuasive. "Eugene Wigner (1969) has demonstrated the fallacy in postulating that life is a physicochemical process which can be explained on the basis of the ordinary laws of physics and chemistry." He goes on to predict "that in order to deal with the phenomenon of life, the laws of physics will have to be changed, not only reinterpreted."[8]

The third objection seems more baseless; there is no tacit theoretical assumption in experimental science that mind cannot act on matter, but simply a methodological assumption that, even if it were to act in that way, it would not corrupt our measuring instruments. Some modern physicists, such as Mach and Heisenberg, began to question the objectivity of matter, and it would probably be fair to say that while we know a great deal about matter, we really do not know what it is. Recent studies, for example, have suggested that psychotherapy might actually change the physical structure of the brain somewhat. Materialists, of course, would argue that there must be some physical aspect of the talk therapy that actually caused the change in the brain-state. This insistence on a physical push is not new or unique to modern materialists. In the Middle Ages, there were those who insisted that quasi-material angels were necessary because an immaterial God can not directly interfere with physical reality. But, in the final analysis, we probably have to admit that we are quite ignorant about the true nature of causality, matter, mind, etc.

The fourth objection is simply a restatement of the authors' response to the very question that we are trying to answer. Likewise, the fifth objection assumes the very conclusion the authors set out to prove.

The sixth objection is perhaps the most ironic of all since Popper and Eccles have devoted so much effort toward showing how Worlds 2 and 3 fit in with Darwinian evolutionary theory.

Nevertheless, Popper and many other knowledgeable thinkers who are favorably inclined to Darwinian theory believe that it may need supplementation.

I have given the seventh objection a good deal of thought but still do not see the analogy between a piano player affecting a keyboard and parapsychology. At any rate, Popper and Eccles agreed not to discuss parapsychology because of its controversiality and the requirements of space and effort that would be involved.

The eighth objection seems to be a rather poorly disguised *ad hominem* argument. Eccles' Christian religious beliefs are of no import whatsoever, nor are Popper's (who was an agnostic and did not believe in life after death). In fact, whether or not science or metaphysics fits in with anyone's religious beliefs is completely irrelevant (as is one's motivations for pursuing truth). If someone is accused of promoting his or her religious views under the guise of science, the only proper response is to show that one's science is really scientific (motives or ends are irrelevant). At any rate, the exact same criticism can be used against physical monism since it supports atheism and can be used to refute other metaphysical views.

WHY IS WORLD 3 NEEDED?

The first question that should be asked regarding the application of the Three Worlds model to consciousness might be why it is necessary at all. After all, if one wants to accept what has come to be known as *folk psychology*, what is wrong with two worlds (good old Cartesian dualism)? This question assumes, of course, that one does not subscribe to either a materialist view (consciousness is reduced to brain states or behavior) or an idealist view (physicality is reduced to subjective experience). But if one accepts the tenets of folk psychology (that human beings possess freedom, intentions, and beliefs that cause our actions) then it is not at all clear why we need World 3.

Indeed, it appears that both Popper and Eccles have argued that World 3 is somewhat irrelevant to the argument between dualism and monism. Eccles, for example, had no qualms about referring to himself as a dualist, and Popper argued that even without World 3, he would still have opted for dualism. He argued that denying the reality of subjective psychic experience is analogous to denying the reality of cats or elephants, and that the reality of World 3 is an independent matter to be considered on its own merits. Popper did insist, however, that the self (but not the mind) is dependent upon World 3.

It seems to me that World 3, apart from any intuitive or self-evident qualifications that it might have, is useful for a number of reasons, some of which have already been mentioned. The acceptance of the concept of objective knowledge helps to unravel the puzzle regarding meaningful connections and causal connections (previously discussed in chapter seven) because World 2 can be causally effective in World 1 but its content leads one to World 3. It also seems that culture is a necessary condition for anything that could be considered human and that is why Popper viewed it as essential to selfhood. And although we may or may not be able to describe the impact of World 3 on World 2 as causal (depending upon one's definition of causality), it certainly does have a tremendous impact on humanity. It is even difficult to imagine human freedom without culturally defined standards of goodness, because the individual would have no guideposts and would simply be the victim of whim, unless perhaps there was some supernaturally revealed ethical knowledge.

World 3 also helps to explain why inner psychic states are not so hopelessly subjective that they can never be compared or contrasted. We are able to empathize with people who share elements of culture with us, and when cultures are very different there is much more difficulty interpreting motives and intentions.

There is yet another reason why World 3 is helpful: the slippery slope that converts dualism into monism. In a monistic universe, either the mental or physical qualities of reality may be lost. There is a difficulty viewing reality as both physical and psychic at the same time and a tendency to incorporate one perspective into the other. Usually this takes the form of physical monism because of the physicality bias. But for some people idealism makes more sense than materialism (physicalism). A pluralistic universe shocks us out of that facile familiarity and forces us to look at the world in all of its complexity. With three realities it may be easier to keep attributes separate, especially since two of the worlds cannot interact directly with one another and require the third as an intermediary. While neutral monism may be compelling from a certain intellectualist point of view, there is more in the world than is encompassed in any one philosophy. Shakespeare (as usual) was right.

NOTES

1. K. Popper, 1994.
2. K. Popper and J. Eccles, 1977, 537–38.
3. Ibid., 548–51.
4. Perhaps these difficulties could be resolved by introducing the concept of potential World 3. The question regarding the ontology of works of art or culture is an enormously complex one. For an excellent discussion, see Nicholas Wolterstorff, 1978. He agrees that a total improvisation would seem to lack the status of a performance or a performance work (p. 194).
5. See M. Bunge and R. Ardila, 1987, 10.
6. K. Popper and J. Eccles, 1977, 541–42.
7. Ibid., 543.
8. Ibid., 544.

Postscript

Why We Cannot Follow Spinoza

This study has included the history of philosophy and consciousness, philosophy of science, psychology, etc. We philosophers tend to view Spinoza as one of the most brilliant and influential thinkers. In the final analysis, however, we must look elsewhere for the popular fascination with Baruch Spinoza. The key may be his first name; it means blessed in Hebrew, as does the Latin name Benedictus, by which he was known after leaving the Jewish community. Spinoza had a unique personality. His needs were few and he strove for spiritual contentment. This and the unprecedented fact that he accomplished those goals outside of any organized religious community may be what most intrigues Antonio Damasio and others.

In the final chapter of *Looking for Spinoza*, entitled "Who's There?" he confronts this issue head on. Was Spinoza really content? If so, how did he achieve fulfillment? How does Spinoza recommend ridding oneself of negative emotions? How effective is his solution? Why was he so ascetic? How can we achieve a "happy ending"? These are not academic philosophical or scientific questions but more like therapeutic ones akin to what is sometimes called philosophical practice.[1] Perhaps they are the original philosophical questions; certainly they were the kind favored by some Hellenistic philosophers. But they are not the kind of questions favored by Plato and Aristotle who, like most modern philosophers, seemed more drawn to abstract and social issues. These are, however, issues that were sometimes addressed by medieval figures such as Boethius and ibn Gabirol. Today they are the kinds of questions favored by psychotherapists or practitioners of Yoga and other meditative disciplines. "Who's there?" is actually a very important question. If there is only one all encompassing substance, as Spinoza believed, there can't really be any individual beings there at all!

Spinoza has become a kind of secular prophet, saint and therapist, all wrapped in one. He offers us an almost superhuman glimpse into ultimate reality. His way of life is exemplary even if few can emulate him. And best of all he delivers the truth that makes one free, truly salvific knowledge. But there is one fatal flaw in that package. The liberating knowledge that he appears to offer in *The Ethics* is the very one that he himself rejected as a political doctrine in his *Theologico-Political Treatise*. In that book he recommends freedom of inner religion and freedom of speech (even though he believed that freedom itself is an illusion). He also recommends government control of external religion and a division of powers between the secular branch of the government and the religious branch—analogous to the kings and priests in ancient Israel. Some say this was an accommodation to the Dutch Reformed Church. But others, myself included, have difficulty in imagining Spinoza concealing his true beliefs.

Nurtured on stories about inquisitions, violent persecutions and forced conversions, he surely recognized that most people are moved not by reason but by emotion. In order to blunt the passions of the mob, a beneficent official religion is needed (one that taught love of neighbor) even if he personally could live happily without any religion whatsoever. History may have proven his *literal* words wrong, at least in the United States. But this is a very religious society with a unifying civic religion; and we must acknowledge that some of the most liberal and tolerant democracies in Europe have state religions even if their populations currently care little about them. And the perceived need for a state religion is even more obvious in the Islamic world, which continues to confound our western secular prejudices. Perhaps the appropriate conclusion, and one that Spinoza would probably endorse, is that societies need some kind of religious foundation because philosophy (and truth in general) is beyond the grasp of the ordinary citizen.

The bigger question, however, is whether his way is a way that most people can appreciate, not to mention emulate. My tentative answer is no. As noted by Damasio, Goethe, in his autobiography, acknowledges his indebtedness to Spinoza with the following words. "But what essentially riveted me to him was the boundless disinterestedness which shone forth in every sentence, 'He who loves God must not expect God to love him in return.'"[2] What a marvelous summation of the neo-pagan ethos! Man can love but God cannot! And does this not fit in perfectly with either a physicalist worldview or an idealist one, such as Goethe himself professed. For both, love is an emergent property, produced by the human evolutionary process.

But the ultimate reality (whether it be physical or mental) is cold and has no love to offer. Therefore, love is ultimately unreal. Humanity's only redemption is in the stoical acceptance of cold inexorable fate or in the acknowledgment that our values are self-produced and not at all anchored in reality. But our civilization has been built upon the crazy notion that ultimate reality is loving and altruistic, giving of itself to all creatures yet not normally revealing its own overwhelming reality (which might threaten our own). And Spinoza, paradoxically, lived his life in imitation of that very modest and beneficent God in whom he did not believe. His actions were exemplary and he seems to have deeply cared about humanity. But if caring is not a part of the truth about ultimate reality, what prevents those of a different temperament from living completely selfish egotistical lives? Ultimate reality would not care! Spinoza remains the austere, solitary figure whose most profound thoughts can never form a basis for the communal existence that gives most human beings true fulfillment, whether they believe in a transcendent deity or not.

This raises profound questions regarding the relationship between purely theoretical speculation and religious or ethical/ political concerns. We have tended to think that the two can be kept strictly separate and I began this study by recommending just that in the area of science. At one time science was a source of human certainty and as such it often came into conflict with religion, which was also viewed as a source of certainty. Many religious people today are willing to admit that their religious traditions contain falsehoods (in the sense of inaccuracies) as well as truths.[3] We also no longer believe that science is certain or infallible; modern scientific theory is always tentative. Yet scientific inquiry still follows its own logic or tradition and must not generally be held hostage to ethical, religious, or political concerns, though there may be certain exceptions to that principle.[4] Likewise, religions do not easily adjust themselves to truths from outside their respective traditions.

But metaphysics is a very different matter. It does not follow any particular logic or tradition; there is no general agreement regarding it but it is an expression of human power, rationality and freedom. It is the original undifferentiated power of Adam to name the other animals while standing under that transcendent reality that it attempts to acknowledge as best it can. The acknowledgment of such a transcendent reality ought to make us very humble (if not modest) regarding our metaphysical pronouncements. And when dealing with such a transcendent reality, the line between *is* and *ought* vanishes. There are no ethical or metaphysical issues that can be completely divorced one from the other because (as Spinoza knew quite well) the ultimately real is also the good. The Western metaphysical tradition has always incorporated political, ethical, and religious concerns just as it has taken into consideration the latest scientific findings. While we can dismiss metaphysical claims as irrational, when we find one that has functioned ubiquitously in many different traditions, humility would move us to grant it respect. As Paul MacDonald concludes in his magisterial study of the history of the mental concept: "with the exception of Epicurus and, much later, Hobbes and Hume, all philosophical accounts of soul connect it closely with an intelligible world."[5] While that may have been an over-statement regarding some of the pre-Socratic philosophers, it is surely true for all post-Socratic thinkers. Hence, we should perhaps be suspicious of those modern thinkers who appear to be in rebellion against that great ethical/metaphysical tradition.

NOTES

1. This movement, sometimes called philosophical counseling, began in Europe and spread to America.
2. See Damasio, 2003, 258–59; or Goethe, 1848.
3. The Roman Catholic Church, for example, makes a distinction between accuracy and truth.
4. One obvious example is the extreme reluctance of scientists to deal with the issue of racial or gender differences in mental functioning, or racial differences in physical functioning. This might strike one as bad science but perhaps can be justified by other overriding concerns. Interestingly, the insistence of some biologists on chance as the only explanation for evolutionary changes is not essentially a scientific position, even if it was the opinion of Darwin. Even if we were to assume that Darwin's theory provides a full explanation for evolutionary changes in living organisms, it does not tell us much about the origin of life itself, nor does it tell us anything about the ultimate basis for the probabilities underlying events in the physical universe. In other words, notions like chance and luck, while useful in everyday discourse, still require philosophical analysis. Such analyses are beyond the ability of most scientists and laymen as they have not been educated in the philosophy of science. For that reason, philosophical concepts are often smuggled into scientific discussions without our even noticing it. Creative design could perhaps be an acceptable *philosophical* interpretation of evolution as long as it does not question what is generally agreed upon as scientific evidence and as long as it does not insist on religious concepts coming out of any faith-based tradition.
5. MacDonald, 2003, 360.

References

Alexander of Aphrodisias, *Commentary on De Anima*.

Allport, A. 1992. "What concept of consciousness?" *Consciousness in Contemporary Science*. Ed. by A.J. Marcel and E. Bisiach. Oxford: Clarendon. 159–182.

Aquinas, Thomas. 1975. *Summa Contra Gentiles*, Book 2. Trans. by J. F. Anderson. Notre Dame: Univ. of Notre Dame Press.

———. *Summa Theologica*.

Aristotle. 1941. *De Anima*. Trans. by in *The Basic Works of Aristotle*. Ed. by R. McKeon. New York: Random House.

———. 1941. *The Metaphysics*, Trans. by W. D. Ross. *The Basic Works of Aristotle*. Ed. by R. McKeon. New York: Random House.

Augustine. *The Confessions*.

———. *De Libero Arbitrio*.

Avicenna. *Commentary on Chapter Seven of Book Lambda*.

Bell, D., H. Raiffa, and A. Tversky, eds. 1995. *Decision Making: Descriptive, Normative, and Prescriptive Interactions*. New York: Cambridge University Press.

Bhaskar, R. 1978. *A Realist Theory of Science*, second edition. Brighton: Harvester.

———. 1998. *The Possibility of Naturalism*, third edition. New York: Routledge & Kegan Paul.

Block, N. 1995. "On a Confusion About a Function of Consciousness." *Behavioral and Brain Sciences*, 18: 227–247.

Brentano, F. 1874. *Psychology From an Empirical Standpoint*. London: Routledge & Kegan Paul.

Brook, A. 1998. "Unified Consciousness and the Self." *Journal of Consciousness Studies* 5, 5–6: 583–591.

Buber, M. 1972. *On Judaism*. Ed. By N. Glazer. New York: Schocken Books.

Bunge, M. and R. Ardila. 1987. *Philosophy of Psychology*. New York: Springer.

Burckhardt, J. 1998. *The Greek and Greek Civilization*. New York: St. Martin's.

Burge, T. 1998. "Two Kinds of Consciousness." *The Nature of Consciousness*. Ed. By N. Block, O. Flanagan, and G. Guzeldere. Cambridge, MA: MIT Press 427–434.

Burke, E. 1757. *Philosophical Inquiry Into the Origin of Our Ideas on the Sublime and the Beautiful*.

Burns, T. R. and E. Engdahl. 1998. "The Social Construction of Consciousness, Part 1: Collective Consciousness and Its Socio-Cultural Foundations." *Journal of Consciousness Studies*, 5: 67–85.

Burnyeat, Myles. 1995. "Is an Aristotelian Philosophy of Mind Still Credible." *Essays on Aristotle De Anima*, Nussbaum, and Rorty, eds. Oxford: Clarendon Press.

Carlson, N. R. 1994. *Physiology of Behavior*. Boston: Allyn & Bacon.

Chalmers, D. 1996. *The Conscious Mind*. Oxford: Oxford Univ. Press.

Crick, F. and C. Koch. 1997. "Towards a Neurobiological Theory of Consciousness." *The Nature of Consciousness*. Ed. by N. Block, O. Flanagan, and G. Guzeldere. Cambridge, MA: MIT Press. 277–292.

Damasio, A. 1994. *Descartes' Error: Emotion, Reason, and the Human Brain*. New York: Harper Collins.

———. 2003. *Looking for Spinoza: Joy, Sorrow, and the Feeling Brain*. New York: Harcourt.

Danto, A. 1964. "The Artworld." *The Journal of Philosophy*, 61: 571–584.

Davidson, D. 1963. "Actions, Reasons and Causes." *Journal of Philosophy* 60: 685–700.

Descartes, R. 1989. *The Passions of the Soul*. Trans. by S. H. Voss. Indianapolis: Hackett.

———. *The Meditations*.

————. 1991. *The Philosophical Writings of Descartes*, volume 3. Trans. by J. Cottingham et al. Cambridge: Cambridge University Press.

Dennett, D. 2006. *Breaking the Spell: Religion as a Natural Phenomenon*. New York: Viking.

Dilthey, W. 1989. *Introduction to the Human Sciences*, volume 1. Princeton, NJ: Princeton Univ. Press.

Dupré, L. 1967. *Encyclopedia of Philosophy*. Ed. by P. Edwards. New York: MacMillan

Evans, G. R. 1993. *Philosophy and Theology in the Middle Ages*. London: Routledge & Kegan Paul.

Fakhry, M. 1983. *A History of Islamic Philosophy*. New York: Columbia Univ. Press.

Flanagan, O. 1992. *Consciousness Reconsidered*. Cambridge, MA: MIT Press.

————. 1997. "Prospects for a Unified Theory of Consciousness or What Dreams are made of." *The Nature of Consciousness*. Ed. by N. Block, O. Flanagan, and G. Guzeldere. 97–110.

Flanagan, O. 2000. *Dreaming Souls*. Oxford: Oxford Univ. Press.

Foreman, R. K. C. 1998. "What can Mysticism Teach Us About Consciousness?" *Toward a Science of Consciousness* II. Ed. by S. R. Hameroff, A. W. Kaszniak, and A. C. Scott. Cambridge, MA: MIT Press. 53–70.

Galen. *Scripta Minora*.

Galin, D. 1996. "The Structure of Subjective Experience: Sharpen the Concepts and Terminology." *Toward a Science of Consciousness*. Ed. by S. R. Hameroff, A. W. Kazniak, and A. C. Scott. Cambridge, MA: MIT Press.

Gerson, L. P. 2005. *Aristotle and Other Platonists*. Ithaca, NY: Cornell Univ. Press.

Ghaemi, S. N. 2003. *The Concepts of Psychiatry: A Pluralistic Approach to the Mind and Mental Illness*. Baltimore: Johns Hopkins Univ. Press.

Gluck, A. L. 1998. "Maimonides' arguments for creation ex nihilo in the guide of the perplexed." *Medieval Philosophy and Theology* 7: 221–254.

Gersonides. 1987. *The Wars of the Lord*, Vol. 2. Trans. by S. Feldman. Philadelphia: Jewish Publication Society.

Gillett, G. R. 1993. "Social Causation and Cognitive neuroscience." *Journal for the Theory of Social Behaviour*, 23: 27–45.

Glickman, J. 1978. "Creativity in the Arts." *Philosophy Looks at the Arts*. Ed. by J. Margolis. Philadelphia: Temple Univ. Press. 145–161.

Goethe, J. von. 1848. *The Autobiography of Goethe: Truth and Poetry From My Life*. Ed. by P. Godwin. London: H.G. Bohn.

Goldman, A. 1992. *Liaisons: Philosophy Meets the Cognitive and Social Sciences*. Cambridge, MA: MIT Press.

———. 1997. "Consciousness, Folk Psychology, and Cognitive Science." *The Nature of Consciousness*. Ed. by N. Block, O. Flanagan, and G. Güzeldere. 111–125.

———. 2000. "Can Science Know When You're Conscious." *Journal of Consciousness Studies*, 7, 5: 3–22.

Gould, S. and R. Lewontin. 1978. "The Spandrels of San Marco and the Panglossian Paradigm: A Critique of the Adaptationist Programme." *Proceedings of the Royal Society of London* 205: 581–598.

Greenwood, J. D. 1988. "Agency, Causality, and Meaning." *Journal for the Theory of Social Behaviour*, 18, 1: 95–115.

Gregory, R., ed. 1987. *The Oxford Companion to the Mind*. Oxford: Oxford Univ. Press.

Güzeldere, G. 1996. "The Many Faces of Consciousness: A Field Guide." *The Nature of Consciousness*. Ed. by N. Block, O. Flanagan, and G. Güzeldere. 2–67.

Habermas, J. 1971. *Knowledge and Human Interests*. Boston: Beacon.

Hamlyn, D. W. 1968. *Aristotle's De Anima Books 2, 3*. Oxford: Clarendon.

Hardcastle, V. G. 1999. *Where Biology meets Psychology*. Cambridge, MA: MIT Press.

Harré, R. 1986. *Varieties of Realism*. Oxford: Blackwell.

———. 1993. *Laws of Nature*. London: Duckworth.

——— and E. H. Madden. 1975. "Causal Powers." *Journal of European Studies,* Vol. 5.

Hospers, John. 1946. *Meaning and Truth in the Arts*. Chapel Hill, NC: The University of North Carolina Press.

Ibn Gabirol, S. 2003. *The Kingly Crown*. Trans. by B. Lewis (with new introduction and commentary by A. L. Gluck). Notre Dame: Univ. of Notre Dame Press.

Idel, M. and B. McGinn, eds. 1999. *Mystical Union in Judaism, Christianity, and Islam*. New York: Continuum.

James, W. 1981. *The Principles of Psychology*. Cambridge, MA.: Harvard Univ. Press.

Jaspers, K. 1954. *Way to Wisdom*. New Haven, CN: Yale Univ. Press.

———. 1963. *General Psychopathology*. Chicago: Univ. of Chicago Press.

———. 1986. *Basic Philosophical Writings*. Ed. by E. Ehrlich, L. H. Ehrlich, and G. B. Pepper. Athens: Ohio Univ. Press.

———. 1957. *Plato and Augustine*.

Jerusalem Talmud.

Keat, R. 1971. "Positivism, Naturalism, and Anti-naturalism in the Social Sciences." *Journal for the Theory of Social Behaviour* 1, 1: 3–17.

King, A. 1999. "The Impossibility of Naturalism: The Antinomies of Bhaskar's Realism." *Journal for the Theory of Social Behaviour* 29, 3: 257–288.

Kristeller, P. O. 1979. *Renaissance Thought and Its Sources*. New York: Columbia Univ. Press.

Kugel, J. 2003. *The God of Old*. New York: Free Press.

Kogler, H. and K. Stueber, eds. 2000. *Empathy and Agency*. Boulder, CO: Westview.

Leonardo da Vinci. *The Notebooks*.

Levine, J. 1997. "On Leaving Out What It's Like." *The Nature of Consciousness*. Ed. by N. Block, O. Flanagan, and G. Güzeldere. 543–555.

Levine, R. H. 1977. "Why the Ethogenic and the Dramaturgical Perspectives are Incompatible." *Journal for the Theory of Social Behaviour* 7, 2: 237–248.

Levinson, J., ed. 2003. *The Oxford Handbook of Aesthetics*. Oxford: Oxford Univ. Press.

Luria, S.E. 1973. *Life, the Unfinished Experiment*. New York: Charles Scribner's Sons.

MacDonald, P. S. 2003. *History of the Concept of Mind*. Burlington, VT: Ashgate.

MacIntyre, A. 1982. "The Idea of a Social Science." *Knowledge and Values in Social and Educational Research*. Ed. by E. Bredo and W. Feinberg. Philadelphia: Temple Univ. Press.

Maimonides, M. 1963. *The Guide of the Perplexed*. Trans. by S. Pines. Chicago: Univ. of Chicago Press.

Malcolm, N. 1968. "The Conceivability of Mechanism." *Philosophical Review*, 78, 1: 45–72.

Marcel, A. J. and E. Bisiach. 1993. *Consciousness in Contemporary Science*. Oxford: Oxford Univ. Press.

Margolis, J. 1974. "Reductionism and Ontological Aspects of Consciousness." *Journal for the Theory of Social Behaviour* 4, 1.

————. 1974. "Works of Art as Physically Embodied and Culturally Emergent Entities." *The British Journal of Asthetics*, 15: 187–196.

McGinn, C. 1989. "Can We Solve the Mind-body Problem?" *Mind*, 98: 348–366.

Menn, S. 1998. *Descartes and Augustine*. Cambridge: Cambridge Univ. Press.

Nagel, Thomas. 1974. "What is it Like to be a Bat." *The Philosophical Review*.

Natsoulas, T. 1978. "Consciousness." *American Psychologist*, 33: 906–914.

————. 1992. "The Concept of Consciousness 3: The Awareness Meaning." *Journal for the Theory of Social Behaviour* 22, 2: 199–225.

Nicholas of Cusa. *De Docta Ignorantia*, II, 9.

Nussbaum, M. and A. Rorty, eds. 1992. *Essays on Aristotle's De Anima*. Oxford: Oxford Univ. Press.

Oatley, K. 1992. "On Changing One's Mind: A Possible Function of Consciousness." *Consciousness in Contemporary Science*. Ed. by A. J. Marcel and E. Bisiach. 369–389.

Peters, Edward. 1988. *The Inquisition*. New York: The Free Press.

Petit, P. 1987. "Verstehen" in *Oxford Companion to the Mind,* Richard Gregory, ed., Oxford University Press.

Philipson, M., ed. 1966. *Leonardo da Vinci: Aspects of the Renaissance Genius*. New York: George Braziller.

Plato. *Hippias Major, Timaeus, The Phaedo, The Republic, The Apology.*

Plotinus, *The Enneads.*

Polangi, M. 1959. *The Study of Man*. Chicago: University of Chicago Press.

Popkin, R. 1979. *The History of Skepticism from Erasmus to Spinoza*. Berkeley: Univ. of California Press.

Popper, K. 1974. *The Philosophy of Karl Popper*. Ed. by P. Schilpp. Peru, IL: Open Court.

———— and J. Eccles. 1977. *The Self and Its Brain: An Argument for Interactionism.* London: Springer Verlag.

————. 1994. *Knowledge and the Body-mind Problem.* London: Routledge & Kegan Paul.

Rakover, S. 1992. "Outflanking the Mind-body Problem: Scientific Progress in the History of Psychology." *Journal for the Theory of Social Behaviour* 22, 2: 145–173.

Randall, J. H., Jr. 1962. *The Career of Philosophy, vol. 1.* New York: Columbia Univ. Press.

Read, H. 1951. *The Meaning of Art.* London: Faber and Faber.

Reed, M. and D. L. Harvey. 1992. "The New Science and the Old: Complexity and Realism in the Social Sciences." *Journal for the Theory of Social Behaviour* 22, 4: 353–380.

Richards, I. A. and Ogden, C. K. 1923. *The Meaning of Meaning.* New York: Harcourt Brace & Co.

Sarkar, H. 2003. *Descartes' Cogito.* Cambridge: Cambridge Univ. Press.

Schmitt, C.B 1983. "The Rediscovery of Ancient Skepticism." *The Skeptical Tradition.* Ed. by M. Burnyeat. Berkeley: Univ. of California Press.

Schütz, A. 1963. "Common Sense and Scientific Interpretation of Human Action." *Philosophy of the Social Sciences.* Ed. by M. Natanson. New York: Random House.

Searle, J. R. 1983. *Intentionality: An Essay in the Philosophy of Mind.* Cambridge: Cambridge Univ. Press.

————. 1992. *The Rediscovery of the Mind.* Cambridge, MA: MIT Press.

————. 1998. "How to Study Consciousness Scientifically." *Toward a Science of Consciousness II.* Ed. by S. R. Hameroff, A. W. Kaszniak, and A. C. Scott. Cambridge, MA: MIT Press.15–30.

Sircello, Guy. 1978. "Expressive Properties of Art." *Philosophy Looks at the Arts.* Ed. by J. Margolis. Philadelphia: Temple Univ. Press. 325–345.

Sorabji, Richard. 2006. *Self: Ancient and Modern Insights about Individuality, Life and Death.* Chicago: University of Chicago.

Spinoza, B. *The Ethics.*

————. *The Theologico-Political Treatise.*

Stubenberg, L. 1996. "The Place of Qualia in the World of Science." *Toward a Science of Consciousness II.* Ed. by S. R. Hameroff, A. W. Kaszniak, and A. C. Scott. Cambridge, MA: MIT Press. 41–49.

————. (1998) *Consciousness and Qualia*. Philadelphia: John Benjamins.

Sutherland. 2000. *Journal of Consciousness Studies*, Vol 7. no.10.

Varela, C. and R. Harré. 1996. "Conflicting Varieties of Realism: Causal Powers and the Problem of Social Structure." *Journal for the Theory of Social Behaviour* 26, 3: 313–325.

————. 1999. "Determinism and the Recovery of Human Agency: The Embodying of Persons." *Journal for the Theory of Social Behaviour* 29, 4: 385–402.

Varela, F. J. 1998. "A Science of Consciousness as if Experience Mattered." *Toward a Science of Consciousness II.* Ed. by S. R. Hameroff, A. W. Kaszniak, and A. C. Scott. Cambridge, MA: MIT Press. 31–44.

Von Rad, G. 1962. *Old Testament Theology*, Vol I. New York: Harper & Row.

Watson, D. R. 1998. "Ethnomethodology." *Journal of Consciousness Studies*, 5: 202–223.

Weber, M. 1949. "Objectivity in Social Science." *The Methodology of the Social Sciences*. New York: Free Press.

————. 1969. *The Theory of Social and Economic Organization*. New York: Free Press.

————. 1978. *Economy and Society*. Berkeley: Univ. of California Press.

Weiskrantz, L. 1992. "Some Contributions of Neuropsychology of Vision and Memory to the Problem of Consciousness." *Consciousness in Contemporary Science*, Ed. by A. J. Marcel, and E. Bisiach. Oxford: Oxford Univ. Press. 183–199.

Williams, M. 1999. "Single Case Probabilities and the Social World: The Application of Popper's Propensity Interpretation." *Journal for the Theory of Social Behaviour* 29, 2: 187–201.

Wilkes, K. 1993. "----, yishi, duh, um, and consciousness." *Consciousness in Contemporary Science*. Ed. by A. J. Marcel and E. Bisiach. Oxford: Oxford Univ. Press. 16–41.

Winch, P. 1958. "The Idea of a Social Science and Its Relation to Philosophy." London: Routledge & Kegan Paul.

Wolfflin, H. 1966. "The Nature of His "Classic" Art." *Leonardo da Vinci: Aspects of the Renaissance Genius*. Ed. by M. Philipson. New York: George Braziller.

Wolfson, H. A. 1977. *Studies in the History of Philosophy and Religion*, vols. 1–2. Ed. by I. Twersky and G. Williams. Cambridge: Harvard Univ. Press.

Wolterstorff, N. 1978. "Toward an Ontology of Art Works." *Philosophy Looks at the Arts: Contemporary Readings in Aesthetics*. Ed. by J. Margolis. [Originally published in *NOUS*, vol. 9 (1975).]

Index